# CHURCH LIFE IN
# THE RURAL SOUTH

A TYPICAL BIT OF THE OLD SOUTH

COMMITTEE ON SOCIAL AND RELIGIOUS SURVEYS

TOWN AND COUNTRY DEPARTMENT
EDMUND DES. BRUNNER, Director

# CHURCH LIFE
# IN THE RURAL SOUTH

A STUDY OF THE OPPORTUNITY OF PROTESTANTISM
BASED UPON DATA FROM SEVENTY COUNTIES

BY

## EDMUND DES. BRUNNER

WITH ILLUSTRATIONS
AND MAPS

## NEGRO UNIVERSITIES PRESS
### NEW YORK

Originally published in 1923
by George H. Doran Company, New York

Reprinted 1969 by
Negro Universities Press
A DIVISION OF GREENWOOD PUBLISHING CORP.
NEW YORK

SBN 8371-1994-4

PRINTED IN UNITED STATES OF AMERICA

# PREFACE

IN the field of town and country the Committee on Social and Religious Surveys sought first of all to conserve some of the results of the surveys made by the Interchurch World Movement. In order to verify some of these surveys, it carried on field studies, described later, along regional lines worked out by Dr. Warren H. Wilson and adopted by the Interchurch World Movement. These regions are:

I.   Colonial States: All of New England, New York, Pennsylvania and New Jersey.

II.   The South: All the States south of Mason and Dixon's line and the Ohio River east of the Mississippi, including Louisiana.

III.   The Southern Highlands Section: This section comprises about 250 counties in "the back yards of eight Southern States." See Wilson, "Sectional Characteristics," Homelands, August, 1920.

IV.   The Middle West: The States of Ohio, Indiana, Michigan, Illinois, Wisconsin, Iowa and northern Missouri.

V.   Northwest: Minnesota, North Dakota, South Dakota and eastern Montana.

VI.   Prairie: Oklahoma, Kansas and Nebraska.

VII.   Southwest: Southern Missouri, Arkansas and Texas.

VIII.   Range or Mountain: Arizona, New Mexico, Utah, Colorado, Idaho, Wyoming, Nevada and western Montana.

IX.   Pacific: California, Oregon and Washington.

Hundreds of people assisted in the survey process, but certain specific acknowledgments are due to those who assisted in the survey of the counties presented in this volume.

The Director of the Town and Country Survey Department for the Interchurch World Movement was Edmund deS. Brunner. He is likewise the Director of this Department for the Committee on Social and Religious Surveys.

The original surveys in these counties were under the direction of the following State survey supervisors for the Interchurch World Movement:

North Carolina: Dr. George Ramsey and Mr. Chester Snell, assisted in these counties by Professor E. C. Branson and others.

vii

## PREFACE

Georgia: Judge H. L. Anderson and Rev. Robert H. Ruff.
Kentucky: Rev. Arthur Stockbridge.
West Virginia: Prof. L. M. Bristol.
Alabama: Rev. R. M. Archibald.
Tennessee: Rev. Dr. Thomas Freeman Dixon, assisted in Blount County by Maryville College students under the direction of Professor A. F. Southwick.
Texas: Rev. Millar Burrows.
South Carolina: Rev. J. A. J. Brock.
Florida: Rev. R. E. Tyler.
Louisiana: Rev. R. E. Cholerton.
Maryland: Rev. Dr. Charles F. Scofield.

Field workers of the Committee on Social and Religious Surveys visited six of the seventy counties included in this study and checked up the information. All parts of the counties were visited and a thorough re-survey was made. Miss Helen Olive Belknap was the field worker in charge of this investigation in all but one county. That one was studied by Miss Elizabeth Hooker. In one county, that of Durham, North Carolina, Miss Belknap's study followed an original investigation by Mr. B. Y. Landis, also of the Committee on Social and Religious Surveys.

The Committee desires to acknowledge its indebtedness to Rev. Robert H. Ruff, Rural Church Secretary of the Board of Missions of the Methodist Episcopal Church, South; and to others from whom he received many helpful suggestions and who made available the results of the survey of the rural churches of forty presiding elders' conferences. The Committee is also grateful to the Committee on Interracial Relations, whose secretaries, Dr. W. W. Alexander and Rev. Robert Eleazar, gave critical attention to the chapter on the Negro rural church.

The technical advisor was Mr. H. N. Morse of the Presbyterian Board of Home Missions, who was also associate director of the Town and Country Survey in the Interchurch World Movement.

Valuable help was given by the Home Missions Council; by the Council of Women for Home Missions through their sub-Committee on Town and Country; and by a committee appointed jointly for the purpose of coöperating with the Committee on Social and Religious Surveys in endeavoring to translate the results of the survey into action. This Joint Committee is composed as follows:

# PREFACE

# CONTENTS

# ILLUSTRATIONS AND MAPS

## ILLUSTRATIONS

xiii

## ILLUSTRATIONS AND MAPS

# CHURCH LIFE IN
# THE RURAL SOUTH

# CHURCH LIFE
# IN THE RURAL SOUTH

# CHAPTER I

## The South—A Goodly Heritage

THIS study is one of a series intended to cover the situation of the town and country church in various parts of the United States. It is a study made from the point of view of the Church; and in the conviction that social and economic conditions directly affect church life. For this reason the early chapters sketch the social and economic background against which will be thrown the picture of the country church in the South.

The Interchurch World Movement's complete survey of seventy counties within the southern region was used as one information source in the preparation of this volume. These counties represent every state in the Old South with the exception of Virginia and Mississippi. From these seventy counties, six were selected, each of which was visited and restudied by a field worker representing the Committee on Social and Religious Surveys. These field workers lived, often weeks at a time, in the counties they studied.

The six counties are Orange and Durham in North Carolina, Monroe in Georgia, Colbert in Alabama, Blount in Tennessee, and Rockwall in Texas. The last-named county is not included in the southern region as defined in the preface; but it has been thought best to include it in this work. Two of these counties, Orange and Durham, situated in the north central part of North Carolina, give a fair picture of some of the regions in which cotton is not raised.

In one of them is a city which dominates the surrounding countryside and which is growing more rapidly than that countryside. The other is the seat of the state university. Monroe County, Georgia, is in the black-soil belt of that state and is famous for its cotton. As counties go in Georgia it is of good size. In this county there has been, during the last decade, a decrease of rural population. In Colbert, the largest of the six counties, both corn and

17

cotton are grown. Besides being agriculturally rich, it holds, in the nitrate resources of Muscle Shoals, possibilities of great industrial expansion.

Rockwall is the smallest county in the biggest state. For an agricultural district, it is densely populated with fifty-eight people to the square mile. Its land is very fertile. It has more wealth per capita than any other agricultural county in the state, and its wealth is chiefly derived from cotton, corn and stock. The last county is Blount, in the mountain region of Tennessee. It contains both fertile valley land and mountainous districts and to that extent is representative of the varied conditions found in the Appalachian counties. It is rich in timber.

These counties exemplify the movements and changes which have taken place in the South during the last century. There have been settlements in all but one of them for a hundred years or more. It is believed that these six counties are fairly representative of the region in which they lie. They have been selected more to indicate the direction in which the South is moving than to stress those retarding conditions within the South which happily are disappearing.

The purpose of this book is to be helpful. It is believed that the situations discovered and the problems disclosed by this Survey will be found so like those in other places as to give far more than local value to certain policies here proposed and programs suggested. And it is to be hoped that the conclusions presented in this volume will prove to be of value not only to churches, church boards and societies, but also to social and educational agencies interested in the general problems of rural religious and social work.

The attention of the reader is called to the fact that towns of more than 5,000 inhabitants have not been drawn upon for the statistical data made use of in this volume.

18

# CHAPTER II

## Economic Characteristics

PRIOR to the Civil War the South was almost entirely rural, and even yet there are more people, proportionately, living in rural communities in the South than in any other part of this country. But while it is still the country "where the corn and cotton grow," the city of Atlanta has increased from 154,000 to 200,000 in the last census period; Birmingham has added nearly 50,000 to its former population of 132,000; and the city of Knoxville, Tennessee, has more than doubled the 36,000 which it had in 1910. These figures are typical of what has happened to scores of southern cities. In every state there has been a steady decrease in the proportion of the rural to the total population, as shown in the last three census periods. In Maryland, Mississippi, and Tennessee there has been an actual decrease in the rural population in the last decade. For the South as a whole the population has increased 30.6 per cent. since 1900; but the rural population has gained only 14.9 per cent. More than two-thirds of this rural gain was made in the first decade of the century. To-day the South is 72.4 per cent. rural. In 1900 it was 82.3 per cent.

### The Riches of the Earth

The South includes nearly one-third of the total area of the Union. It is richer in natural resources than any other equal area in the world. It has three-fifths of the coast line of the continental United States. It produces more than 60 per cent. of the world's cotton. Its natural gas fields are the greatest known in the world. It has the largest sulphur deposits in the world, producing three-fourths of the world's supply. The bulk of the raw materials as well as the factories for aluminum are found in the South. Three-quarters of the coking coal area of America lies within the South. Its coal area is twice that of all Europe, including Russia. Forty per cent. of our forest resources is in the South. Here, too, lie fifty-five million acres of reclaimable land, which could be made to produce crops worth from two to four billion dollars a year. To-bacco flourishes in some sections. In the fields of the South are corn, rice, cane, peanuts, or grazing live stock. Annually it sends several thousand carloads of fruit to Northern and Middle Western markets. From its ports in 1921 $1,867,000,000 worth of goods were exported, a total five times larger than for all Pacific Coast ports. New Orleans is second only to New York as a port.

This is, economically, the South. It stands on the verge of a tremendous industrial development. More, perhaps, than any other

A NORTH CAROLINA COTTON GIN

section of the country, the South will attract industrial enterprises during the coming decade. The Great War marked the beginning of a new period in the history of the South. Wages very greatly increased.

## The Land of Cotton

One important aspect of this industrial expansion is to be found in the rapid increase in cotton-mills. Whole villages grow up about a mill or several mills. The increase in the number of these mills is bringing the Carolinas, which head the list of southern states in the number of persons employed in the manufacturing of cotton goods, into active competition with Massachusetts. The tendency seems more and more to have the mill located near the source of supply. This effects a saving in freight charges and a reduction in cost to the mill owners because labor is cheaper. This labor is drawn largely from the surrounding rural districts; but the cotton-mill village has no direct relation to contiguous rural territory in the sense that an average village has. The people live in an industrial environment that is neither rural nor urban. The homes in these communities are usually the property of the mill owners who often maintain or assist the school, such welfare work as may be carried on, and even the church. There were not enough cotton-mills in the basic counties of this study to furnish ground for any broad conclusions as to the scope and policy of social and church work of the million inhabitants of these villages. Enough mill communities were studied, however, to show in a general way what the problem is.

It may be true, as one woman worker said: "Once a cotton-miller always a cotton-miller." Nevertheless there is a great deal of transiency among the hands. They do not drift to the city, but from one to another of the mills or to the country. Owing to this constantly unsettled condition, enduring church work is very difficult. In one mill, only 2 per cent. of the workers had been there more than four years. In another, about one-fifth had been there ten years; but this was held to be most exceptional. Typical of this phenomenon is the statement of one family in which there were six children:

We * were married at Lake Mill in ——— County. We stayed there about a couple of years, then we farmed about a year. Then we went back to the cotton-mill and stayed about two or three years. Then we went to Woodburg and farmed for a year and a half. Then we went back to Lake Mill and worked about six months and then we moved to Smith County to this mill and stayed here about five years. In the spring we moved back to the Lake Mill and stopped there until Christmas. Then we took to farming for three or four months. We went back to the Hampton Mill and worked about two weeks and then moved to the Triffin Mill and stayed there two years. Then we moved back here and we have been here a year and a half. The last time we tried farming, the man who rented us the land quarreled over everything he furnished us. Then he didn't like our puppies and threatened to shoot them, so we moved.

## Economic Migrations

In times of average prosperity there is little migration from the farms to the cotton-mills. Those farmers who are attracted to the mills are almost without exception tenants. When the peak of pros-

* Their names are fictitious.

perity is reached, families begin leaving the mills to take up farming; but those from the communities studied were all back in the mills again within from three to seven months. Some did not even wait to gather their crops. With the deflation of prices and the spread of the boll weevil, the tide set back from the farm to the cotton-mill, and in 1921 the mills were flooded with applicants from the farms.

Economically, the mills are a help to the South as a whole, for cotton-mill people work at a weekly wage and spend money freely. Said one local merchant: "Without the mills we'd all be busted. The mills keep up the town and the town keeps up the farmer." Wages, however, are not very high: this has been true especially since the collapse of the cotton market, which brought about wage reductions of from one-fifth to one-third. At the time of this Survey, white men received from $1.75 to $2.50 a day and white women from $1.34 to $1.84. Negro men and Negro women received about the same wage, varying from $1.10 to $1.25. Boys and girls earned from $3.50 to $9.00 a week, according to their efficiency.

There is little incentive for the cotton-mill hand to be progressive. He is not permitted to own his own home and is limited to the alternative of working in the cotton-mill or raising cotton. A number of the mills seek to create a social life for their employees, and this policy should be rapidly extended. In the smaller communities, especially, very little is done to improve social conditions. Nor is much attention paid to other matters of general concern. In the communities surveyed surface water came from wells, none of which had recently been analyzed. Typhoid was epidemic at one place. None of the mills had company physicians, although certain doctors were always called in case of accident. There are no nurses or hospitals in these towns. Epidemics once started spread rapidly. Conditions in some of the larger villages are known to be somewhat better.

The Church is doing very little. In fact, it is neglecting some of the mill communities. It must adapt its program to the changed conditions of life of its members who work in the mills; and must take an active interest in the problems raised by the control of communities in large places by industries, or by capitalists who never see the towns in which their employees live and who, therefore, feel little responsibility for conditions.

The South's greatest wealth, however, is in agriculture. In 1920 the value of her crops totalled nearly $5,000,000,000, as com-

Tenancy

Permanency

A STUDY IN BARNS

pared with little more than $1,500,000,000 ten years before. The basic crop of the South is cotton; and as cotton has gone so has gone the South, whose periodic depressions have been caused by the low price of cotton more than by anything else.

Late years have brought a new menace to the agriculture of the South, the boll weevil. Since it gained entrance into this region it has pushed its line of advance farther and farther into the cotton country until now it has reached every cotton-growing state. The destructive work of the boll weevil, made the more calamitous by the dependence of the South so largely on imported foodstuffs, of which as much as $500,000,000 worth was required in the year before the war, has led to a campaign for diversified agriculture. The effect of this campaign is beginning to appear in the census figures. In 1910 cotton was the chief crop in five states; in 1920 it was the chief crop in but four. The cotton acreage, moreover, decreased in virtually every state except Texas. The acreage in corn, on the other hand, increased. This same tendency is apparent in the counties under consideration in this study. In some regions an important stimulus to crop diversification was furnished in the last year or two by the refusal of bankers to lend to farmers who would not sign an agreement to reduce their cotton acreage and diversify their crops.

### Tenancy and Instability

Tenancy presents one of the gravest problems which the rural South faces to-day. It has steadily increased from 39 per cent. in 1890 to approximately 50 per cent. in 1920. While tenancy is more common in the cotton-growing states, it is general in other southern states as well. There are six states in which more than half the farmers are tenants; and in three of the six the ratio is nearly two in every three.

A great deal of the tenancy is, of course, among Negroes; but it exists also among the white farmers to a larger extent than is generally believed. Meanwhile, in a number of communities, Negroes are slowly coming into the ownership of land. At least in the seventy counties one white farmer out of every three is a tenant; and in fifteen of these counties one out of every two. With the one-year lease which prevails, tenancy means a shifting population; and it is difficult to establish or maintain enduring churches or social institutions in counties in which the tenancy rate is high. More than one promising coöperative organization in the South,

THE BOLL WEEVIL DROVE AWAY THE OLD-STYLE FARMER

THE NEW FARMERS' FRUIT DROVE AWAY THE BOLL WEEVIL

and many rural churches, have been laid low by the restlessness of the tenant farmer.

The tenancy system in the South varies. Roughly speaking, there are five plans of farming based on the relation of the farmer to the soil. One is the cropping system in which the "cropper" is little more than a manager and has very little capital invested in the farm. For his labor he is paid one-half the crop. This is the kind of tenancy that has been most commonly written of in articles about the South. The second system, which is rapidly disappearing, is the one in which the renter is the chief manager and capitalist. He pays the landlord one-third of the grain and one-quarter of the cotton as rent.

In a variation of this plan, the tenant pays an agreed-upon part of the product, such as a fixed amount of the crop each year, regardless of the yield. It has been said by several economists that this plan is becoming more general, as is also the fixed money rental plan. Then there are, of course, the small farms operated by part owners; and the plantations where farming on a large scale is carried on and where the landlord as owner and capitalist deals with his help as if they were laborers. Some feel that this system is likely to supplant the "cropper." The original purpose of cropping was to meet the needs of those who were without capital. The landlord was then to exercise control over the farming operations: but, generally speaking, he did not exercise enough supervision to insure success.*

## Agricultural Agencies

The six counties which have been chosen as representative of the seventy, exemplify many of the economic developments of the rural South. All six have had, or still may share, the advantages of a farm bureau and a county agent, and in some cases, a county demonstration agent under the supervision of a farm bureau or, as it is called in certain communities, the County Council of Agriculture. Farmers have been taught to increase production, and have witnessed demonstrations of improved farming methods; problems of marketing have been studied and sometimes solved; classes have been held; fairs or exhibits have been organized; short courses have been put on in the schools for adult farmers; clubs have been formed for adults, but chiefly for boys and girls; and coöperative enterprises have been nurtured.

* "Economics of Land Tenure in Georgia," E. W. Banks.

Such organizations as the Products Exchange of Blount County have been established. Other organizations, such as the Sheep and Wool Producers' Organization, have grown out of the farm bureaus. The Farmers' Union has local groups in a number of the counties; but it is most active in Colbert County. Both the Union and certain coöperative enterprises of the Farm Bureau have been killed by the shifting of population accounted for by the high tenancy rate. Perhaps the most interesting coöperative enterprises are the credit unions in Durham County, one of which has received considerable publicity and illustrates very well the workings of this possibly suc-

A MILL PLAYGROUND, CARRBORO, NORTH CAROLINA

cessful attempt to solve the credit problems of the American farmer.

One of the outstanding characteristics in the rural life of the South is the large trade-area community. The influence of the county-seat town extends farther out into the country in the South than almost anywhere else. Merchants of the counties studied report a far larger percentage of their trade as coming from the countryside than would the county-seat merchants in any other part of the country except the Pacific Coast. The county seat becomes the shipping point for almost all produce raised by the farmer.

## Neglected Opportunities

On the other hand, the southern city does not get very much of its produce from the neighboring countryside. In too many instances the farmers have not yet availed themselves of the neighboring urban markets for high-grade vegetables and dairy products. At present a few farmers peddle from door to door the surplus of the produce raised for their home use; and this, at the best, is a very unsatisfactory practice. It was found, in consequence, that in the city of Durham some of the fresh vegetables reached the stores from as far away as Washington, D. C., nearly three hundred miles to the north.

Whether or not poor roads have any connection with this neg-

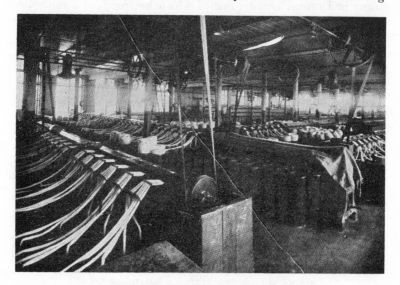

THE END OF THE COUNTRY TRAIL
Many a farm-bred lad finds his way at last into the cotton factory

lect of opportunities is a significant question. "Let's get out of the mud and stay out" is the slogan of one county newspaper in the South; and those few words tell a big story of the condition of the roads in many sections of this area. Having only one or two crops, which can be shipped at a season when the roads are apt to be in good condition, the farmer is more easily satisfied with poor transportation facilities than is the trucker or dairyman who goes daily to a neighboring city. In late years, however, sentiment in the South has been changing. The Federal Road Act, together with bond issues in some states and agitation by automobile and "good roads associations," has led to constant efforts for improved roads throughout the South.

28

# ECONOMIC CHARACTERISTICS

The farmer is coming to see that this improvement will stop some crop wastage, will stimulate trade and bring him closer to markets. During the first ten months of 1922 fourteen of the states included in the southern region floated bond issues for road building amounting to many millions of dollars. North Carolina's issue exceeded $26,000,000, Florida's was more than $7,000,000, and those of five other states exceeded $3,000,000 each. Blount County, Tennessee, has lifted its traffic out of the mire by a bonded expenditure of a million and one-half dollars in the last five years. As roads are improved rural communities will enlarge, undergo perhaps a regrouping, and as a result denominations will have to face the question as to whether or not they have churches of their own competing with one another in the same community. The Survey shows instances of precisely this problem of redistribution; and the reason for it was always found to be improvement in transportation conditions after the erection of the church.

The economic future of the South seems, therefore, to lie along the lines of industrial expansion in the cities, and of diversified agriculture, with better transportation to ensure and facilitate these developments. There remains to be worked out in the South between town and country an adjustment of the labor supply. The South is probably entering the cycle of rural life through which many parts of this country, following New England's lead, have passed. If the South profits by this experience of other parts of the country, it may be able to solve its rural problem almost as it arises.

# CHAPTER III

## Education and Social Life

THE intense economic development of the South during the last five or six years has been paralleled in large measure, where that development has been greatest, by a marked change in social conditions.

In the background of all social life in the South lie two things: the more important is the aftermath of the Civil War and the other is illiteracy. Both of these are disappearing. Conditions resulting from the war produced in the Southern farmer a psychology of discouragement. Reconstruction and readjustment were difficult. He had neither the means nor the time to make use of the social discoveries and experiences of the rest of the country. War was blamed for many things, became a scapegoat for every entrenched abuse, and for every refusal to step forward. This was only natural, for life in the South had to be entirely reorganized; and in the period when the rest of the country was opening up new lands and concerned with new enterprises, the South was unable to forge ahead but had to concern itself with rebuilding its homes and industries and reorganizing its life.

Illiteracy is one of the results of the social situation growing out of the Civil War, though the war can hardly be held entirely responsible for it. In the mountains, poor roads and poverty had much to do with it. The rate of illiteracy among all males over twenty-one years of age varies from 23.6 per cent. in Louisiana to 6.9 per cent. in Maryland. Among white males also these states represent the extremes, the figures being 16.9 per cent. and 3.5 per cent. respectively. For the southern region, the decrease in illiteracy among white males in the last census period has been one-third, the figure now being 7.8 per cent.

### Illiteracy and Tenancy

Illiteracy bears a distinct relation to the economic life. In this connection Professor Branson, of the University of North Carolina, says of certain southern counties: "From one-half to three-fourths of the operating farmers are tenants. Tenancy breeds illiteracy and illiteracy breeds tenancy. Neither can be obliterated alone. The country church must destroy illiteracy and tenancy or together illiteracy and tenancy will at last destroy the country church." Tenancy, with the economic aspects of which we have dealt in the last chapter, is one of the results of the breaking up of the large plantations after the Civil War.

As for illiteracy, and the psychology of depression which has been alluded to, both are rapidly disappearing. Attention is being centered upon these two evils and the net result is a richer com-

COMMENCEMENT DAY BRINGS OUT THE GIRLS' CLUBS

munity life and a rising tide of community consciousness. Improvement is being made in education, health, and general social conditions; and this improvement is well exemplified by development within the half dozen counties which formed the basis for the intensive part of this investigation.

The southern community is not basically economic. From a trade and shipping point of view the county is often a unit in itself. Such a unit is too large for the organization of social life and smaller communities are formed around social interests. Sometimes the boundaries have been set by geographic conditions, as in the mountainous districts; but the social community is apt to cluster around the church, the school, or the little neighborhood store and crossroads senate that often is not open more than part of the time each day. Several states have given to these units the right to

31

organize for certain purposes. These purposes are various. Perhaps a consolidated school is desired, or perhaps a credit union. Except where it is organized for a credit union, a community in the South is much less likely to have an economic basis than is a community anywhere else in the country.

## County and Private Agencies

The dominance of the county seat has fostered a more dominant county spirit than is found anywhere else in America, except, perhaps, in the West; and the county agent movement has tended to strengthen this. In North Carolina a state law now permits every county to have a superintendent of public welfare who, in reality, is the social service secretary for the county. This is just one of the indications of the rising tide of social interest throughout the entire South which is largely the result of the Great War.

The South had, in the war industrial communities and in the cantonments, practical demonstration of the possibilities of recreational and other welfare work. New desires were awakened in the minds of many people; and the possibility of a social life undreamed of before was revealed. Efforts to satisfy these desires and to develop the possibility have been made by wise leaders in some of the states and in many of the counties. The Red Cross assisted in this effort and still in part sustains it. As a volunteer agency, the Blount County Red Cross may be taken as an example. Its work, besides, shows something of the health situation. The Blount County health unit examined more than 2,000 school children for physical defects and found malnutrition, adenoids, imperfect sight or hearing in 83 per cent. Eye diseases and blood-poisoning, often due to the absence of antiseptic precautions, are prevalent and serious. Tuberculosis and typhoid also claim many victims. One of the chief causes of disease is the pollution of the soil and of the water supply. Streams are used as sewers, while springs and shallow wells are not safeguarded. Housing and sanitary conditions have been poor and medical care has been inadequate.

The splendid campaign waged by the Rockefeller Foundation against the hookworm disease throws light on the general situation and shows the necessity for betterment. It is with such problems as these that the Blount County Red Cross grapples, employing a nurse on full-time and a physician for part-time. In addition to this, the Red Cross has formed Home Service Committees, extended relief where necessary, and aided ex-service men and their families.

Durham County, North Carolina, furnishes an excellent example of how to deal with the health problem. There the city and county governments have combined in the establishment of one health department with an efficient staff of workers. It employs a nurse for both city and country visitation; has charge of school inspection; operates a clinic; and is responsible, among other things, for the inspection of dairies, water, and meat supplies. It is doing a highly commendable piece of work which should both inspire like effort elsewhere and receive continued local support.

COMMENCEMENT DAY SPORTS, COLBERT COUNTY, ALABAMA

## Going to Church for Recreation

"What do we do for recreation?" asked one Southern woman, repeating the surveyor's question. "Why, we go to church." What a chance for the church! Of the 138 communities in the six basic counties, only three have moving-picture theaters, two have dance halls, less than half a dozen of the communities have pool-rooms; and apart from the schools there are organized athletics in only seven. A solitary band finds close relationship to three orchestras and six singing schools. One lonely Chamber of Commerce booms its town. Through the influence of the schools, fifteen communities have civic or community clubs and nearly a dozen Parent-Teacher As-

33

sociations. More of the latter are rapidly forming, especially in Colbert County, where it is hoped soon to have a county federation of Parent-Teacher Associations. There are twenty-one women's clubs, three-fourths of them in one county, which also has sixteen girls' clubs under the care of the Home Demonstration Agent. Six communities have patrols of Boy Scouts.

As regards clubs for boys and girls, the experience of West

WATCHING THE COMMENCEMENT DAY SPORTS, COLBERT COUNTY, ALABAMA

Virginia may be cited. There the County Agent, assisted by instructors from the Extension Division of the College of Agriculture, has organized four "H Clubs" among the boys and girls of the state. The four H's stand for head, hand, heart and health, and the children are scored on seven items under each of these divisions, the total possible number of points under each H being 1,000. This scoring takes into account efforts to live up to the Golden Rule, religious training, attendance at church and Sunday school activities. In the summer of 1920, there were twenty-eight camps in the state under the auspices of these clubs, with 1,300 children attending. The program was educational and recreational. These clubs have spread to other states.

In all the six counties there is no public library; but this need is met in part by the libraries in the educational institutions, and the small public school libraries, averaging about fifty volumes, which are to be found in 100 communities. This résumé of the recreational assets leaves out of account that neighborly spirit which permeates most of the Southern communities, and which is responsible for much inter-family and inter-neighborhood visiting, and for other social affairs which are naturally not subject to statistical treatment.

A MODERN PUBLIC SCHOOL IN ALABAMA

## Other Welfare Work

If any one thing differentiates the social organizations in the South from those in other sections of the country, it is the fact that so much of that which is worth while is done by official or semi-official agencies. Elsewhere voluntary organizations care for many needs, but in the South the stirring of social interest has been so recent and the voluntary agencies are so weak that the state has done much which states in other parts of the country have not done and could not do. Just what the result of this will be is an interesting problem for speculation.

The work, however, has had the effect of producing leadership and community spirit. Of the communities in the six basic counties, 70 per cent. have men or women who are recognized as being influential, and even as having determining voices, in matters of common concern. Of these leaders, three-fifths are farmers and one-fifth merchants or business men; the remainder are professional people such as preachers, lawyers, or teachers, or they are women of the community. In a third of the communities that somewhat intangible quality known as community spirit is recognizable, and is evidenced by pride in the home town, by good schools and community improvements.

How necessary it is for the official agencies to furnish all they reasonably can of well-rounded social life is clearly seen when the social resources, apart from those brought by these agencies, are considered.

## The Benefits of Education

The schools of the South are sharing in the new social spirit and there is much to be done. The fight against illiteracy is not over, though it is being won. Then, too, the school is the only public building in which all the people of a community can meet for the discussion of community projects.

As showing what the schools can do, the system in Colbert County, Alabama, may be considered. The schools in this county have made great progress during the last three years under the leadership of Mr. J. T. McKee. The program includes not only school improvement, but also community development through the schools. Four years ago many of the buildings were dilapidated and inadequate. The school term was less than half a year and very few of the children were attending high school. This was due chiefly to the fact that outside the county seat and the city of Sheffield there were no high schools within reach of the majority of the children in the county, and nothing had been done to awaken among the children a desire to go to high school.

The first move of the superintendent was to stress the disadvantage of the one-teacher school. As a result, where there were thirty-seven schools with one teacher each, there are now only eight. Not including four schools which have only the primary grades, there are forty-two white rural elementary schools in the county with ninety-two teachers and almost 3,000 pupils. Of this number 134 are in grades above the seventh. The county high school is located outside of the city. It has thirty-five pupils and three teachers. In addition to the superintendent of schools, there are two supervisors, one of white and one of colored schools, and four attendance officers.

There are now three consolidated schools in the county, while seventeen of the total number of schools have either three or four teachers each. Nine up-to-date school buildings have been built. Each school has been supplied with a map, a globe, and a small library. The expenditures for permanent improvements have amounted to $75,000, which has been raised by a county tax of three mills, with an additional three-mill tax in thirteen special districts.

THE HIGH AND GRADED SCHOOL, CHAPEL HILL, NORTH CAROLINA

The total income for the schools of the county in the year preceding the Survey was $78,000, virtually three times as much as in the school year 1916-17 before the three-mill tax had become effective. Before the present superintendent took office, the schools, almost without exception, had no work above the seventh grade. Now thirty-one have from eight to eleven grades, and nearly every rural child can find at least some high-school work within driving distance. The supervision of teachers has increased and twelve teacher conferences have been held.

Even with so much accomplished, there are still many problems to be solved. Among these are the short school term; the low percentage of attendance, partly due to bad roads and partly to the custom of keeping children at home for farm work; small salaries for teachers; and a tendency among parents to be satisfied when their children have completed the elementary grades. In July, 1920, while 20 per cent. of the children in Colbert's only city or town had completed at least one high-school grade, only 5 per cent. of the county children had; and this represented, for the county children, a considerable improvement over the conditions that had obtained four years before. The superintendent is now stressing the idea that unless a child goes through the eleventh grade he enters life handicapped.

## The Flexible Curriculum

The belief that the school should become a servant to the community is gaining headway throughout this region. New state laws have helped progressive communities and superintendents by allowing the inclusion of courses in hygiene and agriculture in the elementary grades and, along with these subjects, physical education, manual training, home economics and a year of home project work in the high school. In Colbert County, school entertainments are held frequently; and, in many communities, they are the only social events of the year. Meetings and club demonstrations are held in the schools in coöperation with the county agents.

There is a County Field Day and a County Commencement at which blue ribbons are awarded to the best school exhibits. These events are really county reunions. From all over the county the people come in cars, buggies and farm wagons. Fathers and mothers and their children fill the school yards; are proud of their own school exhibit and interested in all the events of the day. The situation in Colbert County is well summed up by the statement of two teachers from Tennessee who were on the faculty of a consolidated school in the western part of the county where the people are largely tenants. They said, "Out where we come from, people love their fine farms, their fine cottages, their beautiful barns and farm implements. Here people do not have all these things, but they are interested in the welfare of their children."

Conditions very like those existing in Colbert County before the present administration still prevail in many counties. The campaign for improvement and consolidation has, however, gained considerable headway. Educational programs such as those in Colbert County constitute a notable achievement, and are rich in promise for the educational and social development of the children of the rural sections of this region.

## What the Colleges Are Doing

In the field of higher education, the influence in the South of colleges supported by religious denominations has been extremely important. Though many of these colleges are small, and though in the past some, at least, did not maintain very high academic standards, these institutions have trained great numbers of young

SWIMMING POOL AT BESSIE TIFT COLLEGE, FORSYTH, GEORGIA

Paid for by the college girls and the town coöperating

people for their life's work. Evidence of the important work done by these colleges may be found in a study of Trinity College in Durham County, North Carolina, and of Maryville College in Blount County, Tennessee. The inspiring influence of Maryville College for over a hundred years, in Blount County alone, can hardly be estimated, to say nothing of its influence in the wide range of country it has served beyond the county lines.

The same statement, except as to age, may be made for Trinity College; and indeed for many other institutions of the same character throughout the South. Finally we should consider the state universities which are making a most valuable contribution to the life of the rural folk and to the entire educational and economic development of the South. Perhaps no university in the South is doing more for its people than the one in North Carolina. Its Extension Department and its School of Social Science reach everywhere throughout the state. Students from its School of Public Welfare have organized community get-together days, with exhibits, games and addresses on the possibilities of rural community life.

Surveys have been conducted that have added to the sum total of social knowledge and furnished the material for further development. Its publications carry the doctrine of community betterment to all who will read; the *News Letter* alone reaches more than 20,000 readers every week, and a study of the files of this periodical reveals the story of pioneer social progress in a great, vigorous commonwealth. Each step, big or little, is carefully reported, and one sees the quiet but very inspiring influence of the leaders of the state university. The communities near Chapel Hill, where the university is located, receive, of course, more attention than those farther away.

What is true of North Carolina is true of many other state universities. The Texas Agricultural and Mechanical College, for instance, has issued several bulletins on rural community organization; and members of its extension staff are devoting themselves to assisting in the organization of local communities. The University of Tennessee also has had a community organization member coöperating with the faculty of its Agricultural College. Peabody School for Teachers has made an outstanding contribution in training rural teachers and community leaders.

Other institutions are developing similar work. The response of the people is remarkable, all things considered. Of course there are failures. Social progress is not a matter of mathematical certainty. There are even dangers in this work lest those who go out from the universities fail to develop adequate leadership in the community and begin the evils of paternalism which rob the local people of all initiative and ambition. But in the main the movement is soundly conceived. It is meeting successfully the real test of approval by the people who continue to support it by taxes. It is one of the most helpful developments in the rural South to-day.

# CHAPTER IV

## The Religious Situation in General

PROTESTANTISM has a strong hold on the South. The number of adherents of all non-evangelical faiths is negligible. They total only about 2 per cent. of the entire church membership; and, except in Louisiana, are to be found almost exclusively in the cities. They form a group that has not increased rapidly. In the six counties included in this study, the number of non-evangelical adherents increased from seven-tenths of one per cent. of the total church membership in 1890 to one and three-tenths per cent. in 1916.

In the South the proportion of Protestant church members in the total population, 40.4 per cent., is the highest in the United States. The South is predominantly rural and its churches are, for the most part, country churches. One-half the rural church organizations in America are in the southern states. Facts like these give exceptional significance to this examination of rural church life in the South. Protestant church membership in the South is significant because of its size; because an increasing number of rural Christians will take themselves to the southern cities as the South expands industrially, just as many have already gone to northern cities; because, in the South, the Church is now virtually the only agency, other than the school, that reaches every community and most of the adults in every community.

What is the Church doing with this opportunity? Out of a total white population of 764,581 the churches of the seventy counties enroll 216,379 people, or 28.3 per cent. of the population. This is a lower figure than one would expect from the regional average, yet it may be accounted for. Both totals include, of course, people in city and country alike. In those six of the seventy counties in which the Interchurch results were carefully followed up, it was discovered that while the urban population was only one-third of the total, the urban church membership was one-half of the total. There are many reasons for this, most of which will be presented later in this study. It may here be said simply that the city church in the South has the advantage of a resident min-

41

ister with services every Sunday. This advantage the average country church does not enjoy.

In the six counties the church membership has increased two and one-half times since the first Federal Religious Census of 1890, and approximately 45 per cent. since 1906. Church membership is therefore increasing more rapidly than the population, which in these counties in the last census period increased only 20.2 per cent. These last figures, taken from the Federal Census, include city churches and town and country churches, both white and colored.

BUILT ACCORDING TO CLASSIC SOUTHERN TRADITION

The Presbyterian Church at Tuscumbia, Alabama

## Denominations in the South

The extent of the country church problem in the South may be readily grasped by a glance at denominational statistics. The South has been Baptist, Methodist, and Presbyterian. No other body has made a very deep impression upon the southern people, if we are to judge by the numbers enrolled, although in the counties which we are studying fourteen other denominational bodies are at work. The Methodists and the Baptists have, however, many more than a majority of the churches.

Throughout the Old South, the Methodist Episcopal Church, South, has 17,000 rural churches, according to the Reverend Robert H. Ruff, Secretary of Rural Work of this denomination. The last figures obtained from the Southern Baptist Convention are given by

Dr. V. I. Masters in his book, "The Country Church in the South." He states that there are 20,000 white country churches belonging to the Southern Baptist Convention. The Presbyterian church in the United States has a few more than 1,000 country churches. The total membership of these groups includes more than four million people; and the churches have an even larger constituency when the children to whom they minister are included. The total white rural church membership of the South probably does not exceed 5,000,000; so that from the point of view of membership these seventy counties have a little less than 5 per cent. of the total church membership.

A COUNTRY CHURCH IN GEORGIA

In this survey, as previously stated, city churches have been excluded. For purposes of definition, incorporated places with 5,000 or more inhabitants have been classified as cities. The churches studied have been divided into three groups, those of town, village and country. Towns have been defined as incorporated centers with from 2,501 to 5,000 inhabitants. Villages include all places with from 251 to 2,500. Hamlets are places with populations of 250 or less and open-country communities are counted as country. In these seventy counties * with their 846 communities, there are 2,415 churches, 135 of them located in towns, 519 in villages and 1,761 in the open country or in hamlets; a total of 2,415 churches or one church to every 319 persons. The six counties out of these seventy have 280 churches in their 138 communities.

* The following chapters discuss the evangelical churches of the white population. A later chapter will summarize the Negro situation as discovered in three of the counties.

The proportion in towns, villages, and country follows closely the proportion for this Southern area with the exception of the towns, for only four of the churches in these six counties are located in the larger centers of population.

## The Abandoned Churches

It is rather startling to notice, however, that in four of these six counties there are abandoned or inactive churches, of which

A COUNTRY STORE IN BLOUNT COUNTY, TENNESSEE

thirty-two have entirely given up their church organization and are dead without hope of resurrection. Twelve more are inactive; that is, they have had no services for a year or more, though each still has a paper organization. Thus, for every seven active churches in these counties, there is one which is abandoned or inactive. A Survey of one-half the rural churches of the Southern Methodist denomination shows only a slightly better result. Ten and two-tenths per cent. of the total number of churches covered in their survey were found to be abandoned. With careful field investigation it is likely that this number would have been even larger, as it is very easy to lose track of an abandoned church.

This increase in the number of abandoned churches, coupled with the fact that many country churches still included among the living are without vital programs or active organizations, has produced another religious phenomenon of more than passing significance. Particularly throughout the poorer sections of the South and among the less securely domiciled elements of the population, various sects stressing the eccentric and highly emotional have multiplied with great rapidity. Included among these are the Holy Rollers and various "isms" and "ites." They thrive where the older evangelical churches have failed adequately to minister to the communities with well-rounded religious programs suited to the local needs, and with sufficient appeal to command the enduring loyalty of the people.

The denominational drives of recent years have had their counterpart in the South, as in the rest of the country; and their influence will appear in any examination of rural religious conditions. The Southern Baptists are devoting very much more time and attention than heretofore to the country community; and their campaign for funds has solidified the denomination more than has anything else in its history. Much the same thing can be said of the Methodist Episcopal Church, South. The fact that in these times collections are difficult does not affect the truth of this statement. The Methodist Church, South, for instance, estimates that for anything like an adequate rural program it must allot nearly thirty million dollars in financial aid to provide for salaries, ministers and programs for the next five years. That the southern denominations are alert, and are thinking in these large terms, is a hopeful sign.

The forces of religion are face to face with a social interest, newly born and still thriving; one which has stirred the imagination of southern congregations. This aroused social conscience is commanding their loyalty and their service, a condition that is quite comparable to a religious quickening. Indeed, the motives which are animating both the leaders of this movement and the students in the public-welfare schools at the state universities are deeply religious. The country church of the South must decide whether it will conserve and even capitalize these spiritual values, or whether it will permit this movement to divorce itself from the Church and proceed independently as nothing but a humanitarian effort.

# CHAPTER V

## Church Membership

THREE-QUARTERS of a million strong are the rural white dwellers in the seventy counties selected for this investigation. The army of the churches is nearly one-quarter of a million; but not all are in active service. Some members have gone beyond reach, are living in other counties, often in other states. Still others, as many as one of every five church members, form what may be called the reserves. The net active membership is but two-thirds of the total, or 143,384. This record, however, is somewhat better than that obtained in a survey of more than 5,000 Southern Methodist churches which gave 61.1 per cent. of the members as active. Furthermore, the membership is rather strongly feminine. Only 39 per cent. of the total are males. It is encouraging to note that one-third are under twenty-one years of age; and in this group again the females lead, though not quite so predominantly as among those members who are over twenty-one.

### Gain and Loss

The South has been well known for its evangelistic zeal; and the previous chapter has noted that, city and country combined, the Church in the South is growing more rapidly than is the population. What then of the country church? The membership rolls of the six counties chosen from the seventy were carefully analyzed with this problem in view. It was found that 205 of the 280 churches added some members to their rolls in the year preceding the Survey; but that only 106, or slightly less than 40 per cent., made a net gain. The total gross gain of all these churches was 2,307 and the loss 813. The net gain, therefore, was almost 1,500, or 9 per cent. of the net active membership.

The largest accessions to membership, 1,742, came through evangelistic meetings, of which 211 were held during the year preceding the Survey. Not all of these, however, produced converts. An analysis of the records as furnished by the churches shows that about 15 per cent. of the meetings were without any result which affected the membership roll. The churches report only 1,628 as coming by confession of faith. The remainder of the gross gain, or 679, was by letter of transfer. It is evident, therefore, that quite a number of converts were former Christians who had ceased to hold an active membership in any given church and whose interest was reawakened by means of the revival service.

## The Sunday School Source

The Sunday school records show that over 1,000 people were brought into church membership on confession of faith; and it is reasonable to suppose, therefore, that the majority of the converts

A POPULAR ALL DAY SERVICE

in the evangelistic meetings were Sunday school scholars who had arrived at the age when they might be expected to join the Church. The net return of these meetings was eight per church. The comparatively small number of people above Sunday school age who joined the Church through these meetings seems to indicate that the evangelistic method, though important, should be supplemented by a consistent, all-year-round program. The results indicate that there should be a very much more intensive cultivation of the constituency of the Church in order to bring to it a far larger proportion of the population than it now holds in membership.

Results of the more carefully planned of these evangelistic campaigns indicate the importance of intensive cultivation. This strategy is to be urged because of the large percentage of inactive members in these churches, a far greater percentage than is found

47

in any other region of the country. Dr. Victor I. Masters, in his book, "The Country Church in the South," says that for every 100 members of Baptist country churches received during a twenty year period, fifteen died and thirty-seven were lost by becoming inactive or through the death of the churches to which they belonged. Coupled with the great evangelistic activity for which the South is noted, there seems also to be a general neglect of the new convert, a failure to nurture the implanted life by adequate religious education, worship, and service.

## The Tenant Farmer Problem

The very evident failure of the Church to reach a considerable part of the population raises a question whether there are any groups that are notably out of sympathy with religion as represented in the country church. It has been found that in the seventy counties white tenant farmers comprise 38.5 per cent. of the total farm-operating group, and only 26.5 per cent. of the total number of farmers belong to churches. If the churches were to reach the tenant farmer as they now reach the farm owner, 4,000 families, or more than 10,000 new members, would be enrolled in these counties.*

In only eight of the seventy counties does the percentage of tenant farmers in the church membership equal or exceed the percentage of tenant farmers in the farm-operating group. When one considers the extent of tenancy in the South, one sees how important it is, not only in respect to membership, but in its bearing on the potential influence of the church in the community. In some of the counties the showing is quite remarkable; and, at the same time, very saddening. In several counties, more than one-half the farms are operated by tenants; yet the proportion of tenant farmers on the church rolls is less than one-fifth. Thus a forward evangelistic campaign among the tenant farmers should engage the combined resources of the Protestant Church in the South.

* A rather extensive study of this subject has been made by Professor L. G. Wilson of the University of North Carolina, and published in his "The Church and the Landless Men." Professor Wilson shows a marked decline in the Church wherever there is excessive white farm tenancy. Tenancy and white illiteracy with their very low ratios of church membership go hand in hand in the twenty-one tobacco and cotton counties of North Carolina. In these twenty-one counties are found more than 26.5 per cent. of the entire non-churched group in the State, though the population of these counties is considerably less than this proportion. In eight of the counties half of the people of responsible age are outside the Church; in one county the church members form only 4 per cent. of the population.

# CHURCH MEMBERSHIP

## Resident Pastors and Membership

Another factor determining gain or loss in church membership is the uneven degree to which the South is evangelized. The proportion of the rural population in the church membership ranges, in the seventy counties studied, from 9.7 per cent. to 57.5 per cent. Within these basic counties there are wide variations from the community standard. One community out of every ten has slightly less than 10 per cent. of its population enrolled in the Church; in one-fifth of the communities, church members form from 10 to 24 per cent.; in another one-fifth, they constitute from 25 per cent. to 33.3

A RURAL PARISHIONER'S HOME IN ALABAMA

per cent.; in about one-half, the membership is over 35 per cent. of the population. This unequal distribution becomes the more significant when it is remembered that so few of these counties have any foreign-born or Roman Catholic population.

One very evident point of weakness in the present situation is the failure of the Protestant Church to maintain its ministry in the more inaccessible parts of the South. In these districts there is, of course, great poverty; and the local people cannot give as much as they could if the soil were more fertile. The proportion of total church membership to population in all these counties is 31.5 per cent.; but in sixteen southern mountain counties the membership is only a little more than one-eighth of the population. In ten of these sixteen it is 25 per cent. or less; whereas of the fifty-four non-mountain counties, there are only eleven in which the church

49

members make up no more than 25 per cent. of the population or less. Similar data are to be found in the variations in active membership between town, village and country churches. Of the town members 73 per cent. are classed as active. Of the village members 70.6 per cent. are active, as compared with 63.3 per cent. of those in the country.

A great deal of this loss may be traced to the infrequency of the preaching services which, in the rural churches of the South, are so commonly held monthly or bi-monthly. Yet such a meager program was the only one by which the southern church could reach its rural population. The social and economic history of this region explains the prevailing system. If, over night, every southern church planned at least one service on a Sunday, there would not be enough ministers to fill the pulpits. All this is true of the present. It is time, however, to consider the consequences. Almost without exception, southern town churches, with their higher proportion of active members, have at least one service a Sunday.

Over one-half the village churches are closed at least one Sunday a month; while of the country churches fewer than one-half of one per cent. have the full time of a minister, and less than 10 per cent. have at least one service on a Sunday. The common experience of Protestant, Catholic and Hebrew has long shown that religious life can be developed and sustained only on the weekly service basis, which, moreover, carries out the tradition of the divine command. Four out of every five churches studied in this survey are guilty of breaking this command. The survey of 8,000 South Methodist churches showed that from 61.6 per cent. to 85.1 per cent. of them were closed on any given Sunday according to the service schedule.

## Size and Distribution of Churches

Another possible explanation of the failure of the Church to reach a greater proportion of the people lies in the fact that the country church is small. In seventy counties there is one church for every 460 men, women and children; but in a number of the counties there is one church for every 250 or fewer. In fact there is, in one case, a church for every 143 people. Naturally, therefore, the churches are small. Because they are small they cannot sustain a preaching service more than once or twice a month. Because they have this service only once or twice a month, they remain small. This is the vicious circle that militates against more rapid progress among the country churches of the South.

This situation makes for what is called overchurching. There are, among the different denominational groups, too few people to provide adequate backing for aggressive programs. But overchurching in the South has about it something of the unusual in that competition between churches in an average community there is confined to fewer denominations than would be the case in some other parts of the country. There are too many instances of church competition within the same denomination whose churches struggle in communities too small to maintain them. However, with the southern tradition of a preaching service once or twice a month, due to an economic inability to support a resident pastor and a large, going church enterprise, overchurching is not the great handicap it might otherwise be.

If, however, it should be possible in a number of communities to consolidate churches, especially of the same denomination, there is no doubt that, with adequate education, a program of evangelization, worship and service could be worked out under resident leadership which might become self-supporting and greatly increase evangelization in those communities. This is something to look forward to, and something which population movements are forcing upon the southern church.

The small villages have been the first to evidence this tendency. In many instances they have come to desire, or are already supporting, a full-time, resident pastor. If this movement continues, as seems likely, church administrators may make the old circuits more compact, recruit ministers for the new policy, and richly serve the South in its own spiritual tradition.

A final feature which seems to condition gain and loss in church membership, also relates to the size of the church. The larger churches incline not only to gain more members per church but to make better proportional gains than smaller churches, both on the one-year basis and on the basis of a ten-year study. The churches in the six selected counties for which there are accurate records showed this to be the case.

GAINS IN MEMBERSHIP BY SIZE OF CONGREGATIONS
ONE YEAR PERIOD

| Size of Church | Number of Churches | Percentage of Total | Number Gaining | Percentage |
|---|---|---|---|---|
| 0–25 .................... | 30 | 10.7 | 7 | 23 |
| 26–50 .................... | 58 | 20.7 | 29 | 50 |
| 51–100 .................... | 97 | 34.6 | 57 | 59 |
| over 100 ................ | 95 | 34.0 | 73 | 77 |
| | 280 | 100.0 | 166 | 59 |

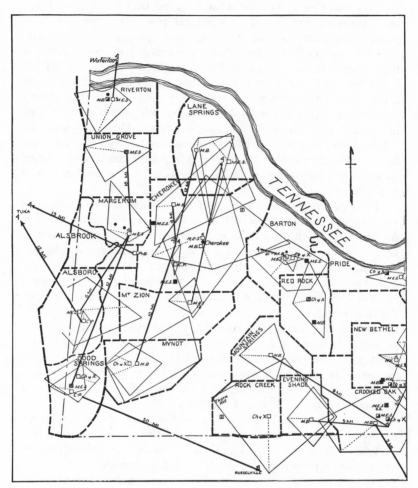

MAP OF COMMUNITIES AND PARISHES IN COLBERT COUNTY, ALABAMA

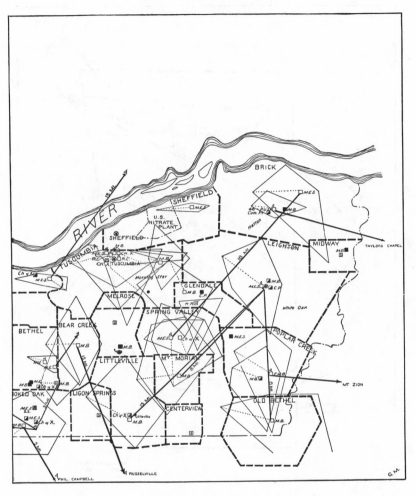

## KEY AND SYMBOLS

| | | |
|---|---|---|
| —·—·— County Boundary | ● Hamlet | ▢──▷ᴬ Circuit |
| — — — Community Boundary | ⊛ Villages | ▢ |
| — — — Neighborhood Boundary | ⊛ Town - over 5,000 | ᴬ Pastor's Residence without Church-White |
| ———— Parish Boundary | ▢ Church -White | ᴬ Pastor's Residence without Church-Colored |
| - - - - Parish & Church Connecting Line | ⊠ Church -Colored | ▣ Abandoned Church.  ▨ Inactive Church |
| ———— Circuit of Pastor | ▢ Church -White with Pastor's Residence | ⑤ Sunday School without Church -White |
| | ⌂ Church -Colored, with Pastor's Residence | ⑤ Sunday School without Church -Colored |
| | | ⊞ Church using School Bldg. |

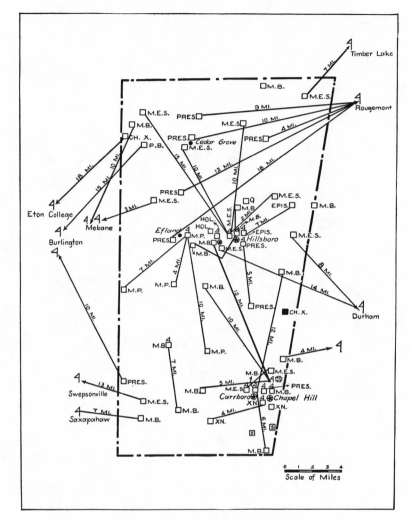

CHURCHES AND CIRCUITS IN ORANGE COUNTY, NORTH CAROLINA

# CHURCH MEMBERSHIP

| Size of Church | Number of Churches | Percentage of Total | Number Gaining | Percentage |
|---|---|---|---|---|
| 0–25 | 16 | 7 | 5 | 31.3 |
| 26–50 | 41 | 18 | 11 | 26.8 |
| 51–100 | 80 | 38 | 48 | 60.0 |
| over 100 | 77 | 37 | 62 | 80.5 |
| | 214 | 100 | 126 | 58.8 |

The Southern Methodist Survey showed very much the same situation. This study covered 5,300 churches. Of those with fewer than twenty-five members each, 41 per cent. were increasing; in the group with the membership between twenty-six and fifty, 54.5 per cent., and in the group between fifty-one and one hundred, 63 per cent. showed an increase; in the group with 100 to 149 members an even 80 per cent. were forging ahead; while, among those congregations with more than 150 members, 90.1 per cent. were increasing.

## Church Parishes

Maps showing the church and community boundaries for three of the six counties illustrate the methods used. The parish boundaries have been drawn to show the average area covered by the Church. In many counties in which the roads are good, and where the communities are not only heavily populated but close together, church parish boundaries are difficult to determine because the personal choice of the people largely enters into their selection of a church. Within the good-road area of the counties the majority of the people can reach more than one Protestant church of their own denomination in less time than the average church member in a large city can get to his downtown church. The parish boundaries, therefore, have been drawn to show the average area covered by a church, and exceptional cases have been eliminated as far as possible. The procedure used was to follow down each road leading to the church and locate the home of the last regular attendant living within a reasonable distance. The outside points on each road were then connected by straight lines.

The maps show typical conditions. They show how pastors are concentrated in the county-seat town or in the larger centers of population; they also show the unevangelized areas. In the study of the seventy counties, it was discovered that one community in every seven did not have a church. This was the situation, however, in only half of the counties. This half included almost all those located in the southern mountain region, though several were in Florida. The remaining communities were scattered throughout the rest of the counties.

## CHAPTER VI

## Shepherds of the Flock

SUBSEQUENT chapters will show that the program of the Church in the South is primarily a preaching program. Very little else is attempted. Buildings are erected chiefly to provide auditorium space for the congregations. But improvement in the general situation of religion in the rural South must come by way of the minister.

A MOUNTAIN CHURCH IN TENNESSEE

The 2,415 churches studied are served by 1,357 ministers, an average of one minister to every one and three-quarters churches. Even this average is better than one might expect who had heard tales of the exceedingly large circuits served by the southern minister. It should be recalled, however, that many of the ministers are men engaged in other occupations by which they eke out a mere pittance; these are the so-called "toiler-preachers" who are expected to devote no more than the Sunday to the work of the church, and who generally receive only a nominal compensation for their work. Such a man, as a rule, serves only one congregation. Ministers giving their full time to their profession serve on the average some-what more than two congregations each.

## The Circuit Rider

In the South, more than in any other part of the United States, the pioneer tradition of the non-resident minister has persisted. The

TWO LOCAL PREACHERS IN ALABAMA

circuit rider is made responsible for the care of a number of preaching points, and travels from one to another, visiting each but once or twice a month and staying only long enough to preach a sermon and, now and then, to conduct a Sunday school. In certain of the less-favored agricultural areas the minister is not even available for funerals, but funeral services are held at infrequent intervals for all who have died since the last pastoral visit.

Full-time resident ministers serve barely 20 per cent. of the

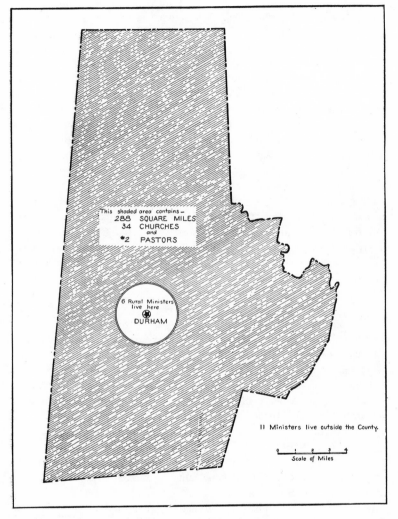

This shaded area contains—
288 SQUARE MILES
34 CHURCHES
and
#2 PASTORS

6 Rural Ministers live here
DURHAM

II Ministers live outside the County.

0 1 2 3 4
Scale of Miles

DURHAM COUNTY, NORTH CAROLINA

churches in the seventy counties surveyed. Almost as many of the ministers of the South serve two churches; 22 per cent. serve three churches; 38 per cent. have four or more, which often means five, six, or even twelve churches. The surprising thing in these situations is the size of some of the churches on these circuits. Their memberships are often more than a hundred and not infrequently exceed two hundred.

But the long habit of the South must be remembered in this connection. All denominations are working to reduce circuits; and progress is being made as more men are available and the people come to see the advantage of having a resident pastor. The economic situation has also had an influence. With the low income that was the lot of the southern farmer for a generation or more after the Civil War, the support of a full-time pastor was not so feasible as in the rest of the country. But conditions have improved. Of the town churches 46 per cent. have the full time of a resident minister and an additional 19 per cent. have a part-time resident. For the village churches the figures are 15 and 34 per cent. respectively; but of the country churches only seven out of 1,761 have full-time resident ministers. Nine per cent. have part-time resident pastors.

## The Absentee Pastor

Only 7 per cent. of the churches in the six basic counties have the two preaching services a Sunday which are customary in many other places; and only 9 per cent. more have one service each Sunday. Four-fifths of the churches have either one or two services a month, while 3 per cent. have services less frequently than once a month. In 1915, according to "The Country Church in the South" by Dr. Victor I. Masters, there were 36,500 country churches in the southern states; and of these 80 per cent. were served by absentee pastors, and 90 per cent. had preaching only once a month. In other words, on any given Sunday virtually 27,000 country churches in the South are closed. "It is only by courtesy that we may speak of these absentee preachers as a 'pastor' in the New Testament sense of that term. As a shepherd of the flock he is an absolute nonentity," says Dr. Masters, who condemns the whole system in sweeping terms.

The South must learn that the absentee minister is a type of the past. He is less efficient than the man who is on the job day in and day out, and who shares all the community interests and activities. The resident minister is interested in the community's schools because his children attend them; is zealous for clean recreation because he wants them and their young friends to have it. As a resident, he is available with spiritual solace in times of bereavement or distress. Of the 138 communities in these counties only twenty-eight have resident ministers, while 110 are pastorless.

Examples of this situation will point the evil. In Durham County only two ministers live in the 288 square miles outside the city in which there are thirty-four churches. One serves six different points, while the other does not live in his parish, but five miles away. The remaining twenty-seven churches are served by seventeen preachers, of whom six live in the city of Durham and eleven outside the county. Blount County, which includes one section with an area of nearly 300 square miles and a population of 6,709, has forty churches, none of which has a resident minister.

Some of these ministers travel as far as fifty miles to reach their appointments. One out of every four churches has a minister who lives more than ten miles distant. In a number of cases, as will be noted on the parish map, the minister lives outside the county in which his church is located; while there are ministers living in the six counties who serve fifty-nine churches lying outside the counties in which they reside. With such conditions obtaining it was not surprising to find that one-tenth of the churches were pastorless at the time of the Survey.

It has been stated that spiritually and materially the full-time resident pastor is a paying proposition. And it is interesting to note that of the churches served by full-time resident ministers, 78 per cent. registered a net gain in the last decade as well as during the year preceding the Survey.

## The Rewards of a Full-Time Pastor

Of those churches without full-time, resident pastors only 52 per cent. gained in membership last year, while in the last decade only 41 per cent. showed an actual increase. The difference, however, as between 78 per cent. and 41 per cent. is not nearly so significant as is the amount of gain; for the average net increase in church membership of those congregations with resident ministers was 50 per cent. greater than the increase of those congregations with nonresident ministers.

A resident minister also has a very real effect upon church finance. In the town and village churches, the per capita contribution in those congregations with resident ministers was $17.88 annually; while in churches with non-resident ministers the average contribution per member was $9.05 a year. In the open country the difference was almost as striking: the churches with resident ministers averaged $11.57 per member as against $7.23 per member for churches with non-resident leadership.

THE PRESBYTERIAN CHURCH, CHAPEL HILL, NORTH CAROLINA

For all the churches of the six counties, those of town, village and open country, the average per capita contribution of the congregations with *full-time* resident ministers was $18.24; of those with *part-time* resident ministers, $15.71; while for churches with *non-resident* ministers the amount fell to $8.00 per member. In every county the figures favor the resident minister.

The Colbert County town and village churches, with an average of nearly $25 per active member where there was a resident pastor, and those of Durham, with an average of nearly $23 per member, show also that there is no economic reason why an average-sized congregation in the South should not avail itself of the full time of a trained man.

The resident minister almost always means a well-organized and up-to-date Sunday school, as well as better equipment and increased influence for the Church in community affairs. Though the organizations are few, even for women, in the southern country churches, and though the program is meager, what work there is along these lines is largely in the churches with resident ministers. Still other factors indicate the desirability of a larger measure of pastoral care for southern country churches, and will be considered in the chapter on church membership. Furthermore, it is to the advantage of the pastor to serve but one church or, at the most, two. Not only can he do more lasting work, but he is better paid. The salary most frequently paid to ministers serving one church is exactly 100 per cent. higher in these seventy counties than that of the minister serving two or more churches.

## Educating the Pastor

Of recent years the broader training of ministers has been receiving widespread attention in the Protestant Church. In response to this need throughout the country both secular and denominational colleges and seminaries are offering, during the summer semester, post-graduate and extension courses for the country ministers. Among other denominations the Methodist Episcopal, South, has embarked upon a progressive educational policy that provides more than a dozen schools for its pastors who have not had the advantages of college or seminary training. This service has reached about 1,000 rural pastors, and includes a correspondence course for those unable to attend the summer course at one of the institutions.

This is a masterly effort to solve an urgent problem; for, as a rule, the services of a man of college training are at a premium. He is called to the largest church, and his church invariably registers the greatest advances in work, membership, and finance. "To him that hath shall be given." From this point of view it is interesting to notice the leadership of the churches in these counties. Seven out of every ten of the ministers have had no college or seminary training. Only 11 per cent. have had both, and about one out of every five has had some college work. The average country minister in the South has to his credit sixteen years of arduous service; but this period represents service in about eight different pastorates. Barely has he become acquainted with his congregation and put a program into effect when he is ready to move elsewhere.

In the Southern Methodist Church the average pastor has had 13.2 years of experience; but his average stay in each charge has been only two years. This is a considerable handicap. The minister should take time to get .acquainted with his people, to understand their spiritual life, and to win their confidence before he can serve them to his best ability. Otherwise they fail to repose complete confidence in him. In our six basic counties only twenty churches have retained their present pastors through the last decade, a little more than twice that number have made two changes. Ninety-six churches divided almost equally the services of three or four ministers during the last ten years. Thirty-nine have listened to five different preachers each, six to twenty each, seven to eight each; eight churches have each seen ten men come and go, while the remainder have had bowing acquaintance with one or more ministers per year. Thus, more than three churches out of every four have retained their ministers only three years or less; and over half have had an average pastorate of two years or less, allowing for the time the pulpit was vacant between pastorates.

### The Laborer and His Hire

One reason for these ministerial migrations lies in the custom which obtains in one of the two largest denominations of the South and in several of its smaller bodies: the pastors are changed every few years. Another reason, however, may lie in the inadequate salaries. The exact situation in the seventy counties, of ministers giving their full time to religious work, is shown in the following table:

| Salary Received by Minister | With No Other Occupation | |
|---|---|---|
| | Serving One Point | Serving Two or More Points |
| No salary | 20 | 53 |
| $500 or less | 30 | 46 |
| $501 to $750 | 4 | 35 |
| $751 to $1,000 | 16 | 84 |
| $1,001 to $1,250 | 28 | 90 |
| $1,251 to $1,500 | 29 | 64 |
| $1,501 to $1,750 | 25 | 61 |
| $1,751 to $2,000 | 8 | 36 |
| $2,001 to $2,500 | 37 | 21 |
| Over $2,500 | 12 | 5 |

These figures include $250 added to the cash salary as the estimated rental value of the parsonage whenever it has been furnished to the minister. It will be seen that some of the churches are beginning to pay an adequate wage in return for the best efforts of a pastor and are therefore attaining adequate results.

There are only 630 parsonages in the seventy counties, and even some of these are not occupied, as ministers prefer to live in the county seat both because of its greater advantages and because of its convenient location for reaching a larger number of their congregations. Too often the minister does not cast his lot with his people as does the missionary on the foreign field. Whether this is the fault of the minister or of the congregation or of the system cannot be determined. Thus 464, or 54 per cent. of the communities, are without resident ministers, while nearly 80 per cent. have no minister who gives his full time to the cause of Christ in the community.

There is a disturbingly large number of ministers who have other occupations. In fact 48.1 per cent. of the ministers in the seventy counties depend on farming, teaching, or business for part of their income. Two-fifths of these ministers confine their services to just one church; and another fifth have only two churches. The rest have three or more churches. The church with a minister engaged in another occupation besides that of the ministry is, however, no better off than one that has to share its leader with other congregations. No other region has so many ministers with other occupations as has the South. Except for the Southwest, largely churched by southern bodies, there is no other region in which more than 15 per cent. of the ministers are engaged in other occupations.

Nearly all of the ministers in the seventy counties, except some in town or village, are compelled to use some form of conveyance. Almost all of them must furnish their own conveyances and pay for the upkeep. The churches of the South, indeed all circuit churches, demand that the minister be an itinerant—a sort of traveling salesman of sermons. But unlike the salesman for a commercial house, he does not have his traveling expenses paid. One denomination in the South has discovered that for 2,000 ministers whose work necessitated travel, the annual transportation bill was nearly $400,000. Seventy per cent. of these ministers use automobiles, 20 per cent. of them use horses, and the others use the railroad. The average transportation expense was $223, $146 and $88 respectively for these three groups—surely a heavy drain on the slender income of the pastor.

The ministers and church members in the six basic counties are fully aware that the churches are facing very grave problems. The most frequent complaint of the church members is of a lack of leadership on the part of ministers. Pastors, on the other hand, complain of indifference and lack of leadership among their local workers. Ministers and laymen alike are aware that under the itinerant plan there is no time to develop leadership, no opportunity to relate religion to life, and no possibility to make the Church felt as a dominating influence in the local community. They all admit that in a state-wide movement, such as the prohibition campaign, which touched the emotional convic-

BIRTHPLACE OF HELEN KELLER, TUSCUMBIA, ALABAMA

tions of the people, the Church was a considerable factor. Sectarian differences which divide communities and hamper community spirit, overchurching, small memberships, illiteracy and the shifting of population have been mentioned as handicaps.

Despite these handicaps, however, the general attitude of the people is optimistic. When asked as to the outlook for the future, twenty-nine churches reported it *very good* and sixty-two thought it *good,* making approximately one-third of the churches surveyed confident of their future. Nearly another third considered the future as *quite fair.* A final third reported it *uncertain and poor.* This third includes the majority of smaller churches, and many of those receiving Home Mission Aid. Despite the optimism disclosed, the fact remains that the members of these churches have not devoted much thought to the future of the Church in their counties.

# CHAPTER VII

## Equipment and Finance

THE data on equipment and finance here presented relate only to the six counties selected for intensive study.

Of the 280 church organizations in these counties 259 own buildings, and the other 21 worship in school houses, stores or halls. Ninety per cent. of these church-owned buildings are of wood, and four out of every five have only one room and are lighted by oil lamps. One-tenth of these churches are in poor condition while an equal number are reported *very good*. The great majority are, however, classified as fair. Fourteen of the larger churches have two rooms, twenty-two have from three to five rooms, a dozen from six to nine, and four churches have ten or more rooms.

The total seating capacity of the auditoriums is sufficient to accommodate two-thirds of the population. It will be seen, therefore, that even the one-room buildings are adapted to seat the largest audiences that ordinarily assemble on the most important occasions, such as fifth-Sunday meetings or evangelistic services. The average seating capacity of a church is 245. No church among these 280 has any social equipment except an occasional kitchen, and except also one stereopticon and a victrola possessed by one of the churches.

Virtually the same results were obtained in a study of nearly 8,000 Southern Methodist churches, 86.3 per cent. of which had but one room. Four and five-tenths per cent. had two rooms. Nine and two-tenths per cent. had from three to five rooms.

It becomes apparent that the chief function of each of these churches is to furnish auditorium space for an audience. Little else apparently is expected. The program is a preaching program. The one-room building is not well adapted for any modern religious educational program.

### The South Pays Its Share

The financial records of the churches in the South are very good when the program, equipment and administration are considered. With so large a proportion of the country churches on a once-a-month preaching schedule, it is hardly to be expected that the rate of giving will be high; and indeed the contributions do show a direct relation to the amount of pastoral service a congregation receives. It should also be stated that in recent years church contributions have increased throughout the South; and that while the collapse of the cotton market seriously affected the church receipts during the year of the Survey, nevertheless the South shared in the general advance, especially in benevolent giving, which has taken place throughout the United States during the last five years.

The Southern Methodists, for instance, during the last year contributed for their Centenary and Educational Campaigns approximately twenty million dollars on five-year pledges aggregating seventy-five million. The Southern Baptist benevolences for home and foreign missions have increased from less than a quarter of a million dollars thirty years ago to nearly a million and three-quarters at the time of the last religious census in 1916, since which time this denomination has had its receipts materially increased through its Forward Movement.

Several factors enter into the amount of per capita giving. In these six counties it averages $10.52 per member a year. The town and village churches better this record by more than 58 per cent. in churches with resident ministers, and about 25 per cent. in churches without resident ministers. In the open country the average is lower; but this may be accounted for by the small amount of ministerial service which these churches receive as compared with the service received by those at the center.

Another factor is the economic environment of the church. Those located in the mountain and hill sections of Blount and Colbert counties, where the soil is poor and the marketing of products is difficult and expensive, average but $5.62 per member a year, which is only a little more than half the total average per capita giving in these two counties.

An adequate financial system also plays a most important part.* Many of the churches are adopting modern methods of church finance. Seventy-eight of them budget all monies, and fifty-two more budget their local expenses one year in advance. Almost half the churches, therefore, are familiar with the operations of a budget system. Of the 160 churches using this system in some form or

* See definitions in Appendix.

other, 108, or 73 per cent., have an every-member canvass, and sixty-six use the weekly envelope system.

One-quarter of the churches, therefore, have adopted the entire system of church finance now most approved. The results of this system are clearly apparent. The churches that use in their financial organizations at least two of the three component features of the modern system, contributed to all causes an average of $10.75 per member a year. Those with no financial system averaged only $8.00 per member a year. In some counties the difference is not very large, notably in Blount, where virtually all the churches are in the open country and where mountain conditions prevail. In other counties, however, the range is much larger. In Colbert, for instance, the difference in favor of an adequate system as against haphazard methods is nearly threefold.

In the year preceding the survey the 270 churches that keep financial records raised $186,722.30. The forty-seven town and village churches among these accounted for a little more than half this sum with their average of $2,010.80 per congregation. This compares quite favorably with the average receipts for town and village churches in other regions. On the other hand, the average expenditures for all causes in the country churches were $413.52 per congregation, which is the lowest average for any region in America. This may be accounted for by the handicap of the absentee pastor, and by the general economic situation.

## Receipts and Expenditures

In this discussion of the financial methods of the churches it is interesting to note that of all the money raised in the town and village churches 70 per cent. was by subscription. Twenty-seven per cent. was from collections and 3 per cent. was raised in various other ways. In the country congregations only three-fifths of the money is raised by subscription, while nearly one-third comes through plate collections, and 1 per cent. in other ways. Of all the money received 42 per cent. goes to the ministers in salaries, 37 per cent. is contributed for benevolent purposes and 21 per cent. is apportioned for new buildings, up-keep and miscellaneous expenses.

The proportion of money given to benevolences is high. Prior to the Great War it was the exceptional country church which gave as much as 25 per cent. of its income to others. The effect of the recent denominational drives, and probably a surviving effect of the war campaigns, have raised the level of giving, and especially benevolent giving, so that it is not unusual, in whole counties, for the churches to donate an average of from one-quarter to one-third of their income to benevolent causes. A record of 37 per cent. for a group of half-a-dozen counties is unusually good.

It should be stated, however, in regard to this record that it is easy for a church whose budget averages less than $500 annually, and which has a non-resident minister and therefore small overhead expense, to maintain a high proportion of benevolent giving which may not necessarily indicate high per capita offerings. This is true of the South, whose average per capita offering of a little over $10.00 is low. The second factor contributing to this high proportion of benevolent giving is the exceptionally good work being done in certain of the town and village churches which have progressive congregations and resident pastors with missionary vision.

## Home Mission Aid

In the United States one church out of every six in the town and country region is helped by the national, state or district home mission aid. In the six basic counties under survey, forty-five churches, or approximately 16 per cent., which is almost the same as the percentage elsewhere, received aid. This aid averaged $283.30 per church a year. Some of these churches have been aided for more than fifty years, and slightly more than one-third of them have received this assistance for over a decade. Nearly three-quarters of those aided compete with other churches; and in quite a number of these cases the competition is with a self-supporting church of the same denomination. The thirty-three aided churches which are competing with others in their communities are given slightly more aid per church than are the remaining dozen which have a clear field and which are the only religious institutions serving their communities. It will be seen, therefore, that nearly $10,000 of the $13,000 expended in such aid is given more to sustain a denominational group than to sustain the ministry of religion in a community which would otherwise be without such service.

This system of aid is obviously wasteful. The South, in common with other parts of the country, needs a redefinition of the expression "Home Mission Aid" in terms of the larger purposes of Him who knows neither "bond nor free, male or female, Jew or Gentile." Its new meaning would bring the churches to realize that the new needs arising in the South call for a pooling and a strategic direction of their precious resources instead of wasteful, futile competition and overchurching. There is a city-ward drift of population which will create a need for churches of a new type in many of the industrial centers. There is need of support for an adequate ministry in the less favored agricultural sections, and for a church that will minister more richly and variously to its community than do most of the churches under consideration. There are communities that are without churches and that need attention.* Moreover, the South cannot continue to avoid its duty to the foreign-born immigrant. One-third of the unnaturalized inhabitants of the United States are on the land, and there are signs that the coming decade will bring an increase of foreign-born settlers to the farm lands of the South.

The financial situation of the churches therefore holds warning of danger yet inspires hope. If the Church develops a program that will let it keep pace as the South advances, and if its proportion of missionary giving is maintained, Southern Protestantism will become one of the greatest factors in world evangelism. On the other hand, if the South is content to give to religion on the basis of about twenty cents a week per member, no great progress on the part of the church can be expected. It is not too much to demand such progress from the church of the South. Studies made by the University of North Carolina Club show that its own state is spending ten times as much on luxuries as on education and religion. Under such conditions the Church has the right to call its membership to a deeper consecration of its resources to the essential purposes of Christianity.

---

* Of the Southern Methodist rural churches 12.8 per cent. were receiving home mission aid. Many of these were in the sort of communities listed above, as needing aid. The extension program, regarded as necessary by this denomination, has already been mentioned.

# CHAPTER VIII

## Church Program

PREACHING is the overshadowing feature of the Southern Country Church program. With only this in view the church buildings are planned, the various religious activities are scheduled. And yet, as has been shown in the foregoing pages, four out of every five churches in the South are closed, as far as the holding of regular services is concerned, on at least one Sunday a month; while figures presented by Dr. Masters for the Baptists, and by the most recent rural church survey by the Methodists, indicate that on any given Sunday two out of every three of the rural churches in the South are closed.

In fact, one-fourth of the total number do not even have Sunday schools. Despite this indifference and neglect, the Sunday school is of the greatest importance to the country church. In seventy counties, with a total of 1,657 schools, whose aggregate membership is a little over 121,000, the town schools average 187 pupils, the village 85, and the country 58. In town and village the average attendance is just a little less than two-thirds of those enrolled, but in the country it is 71.2 per cent.

### The Sunday School

In a detailed examination of the church program based on the six typical counties, the Sunday schools incline to the same sort of program that characterizes the churches. The lessons are taught in a perfunctory way. The scholars are given no other activities to absorb their interests and energies. For instance, in the country only the exceptional Sunday school makes mission study a definite part of its school work, though 40 per cent. of the village Sunday schools do include a certain amount of such work. Only one-third of the schools so much as take up regular missionary offerings; only seven observe Decision Day; and but three have classes to prepare for church membership. These three are in some of the very strongest of the churches. It is not surprising, therefore, that only 110, or less than half the Sunday schools, sent pupils into church membership; and they sent a total of 1,034.

The village Sunday schools have an average of two and one-half pupils each pursuing their regular studies beyond high-school grade. The country Sunday schools average one each. There are only thirteen teacher-training classes, eight of them in villages. Nine more schools attempt some sort of leadership training. For other activities, only twenty Sunday schools, twelve of them in the villages, have organized classes. Only about one Sunday school in twenty has a home department and only about one in ten a cradle roll. One of the most serious features in the situation is that of the 223 Sunday schools only 147, or a scant two-thirds, keep open the entire year. Poor roads chiefly are responsible for this.

In the last ten years, fifteen Sunday schools have sent twenty-three pupils into professional Christian service. Three of the six counties have not sent a single candidate during the last decade. Twelve of the twenty-three sent into service are products of schools in Orange County and largely of those in Chapel Hill, where, it will be recalled, the state university is located. In view of the fact that Protestantism has virtually no competition in the South, and that religion in the South has been noted for its fervor and its deep emotionalism, this record is both surprising and alarming. There are single counties on the Pacific Coast where materialism is supposed to have full sway and where church membership numbers but one-tenth of the population, that have sent at least as many young people into Christian service in the last decade as have these half dozen counties put together. It is hard to fix upon any one thing as accounting for this.

## Contributory Causes

But the situation is not beyond remedy. Poor schools have something to do with it. The Church program, meager to the vanishing point, is another factor, since it makes no appeal to virile young men and women who judge the Church by what they see. In support of this view is the fact that the majority of those who have gone into Christian service have come from the strongest congregations.

The South has rewarded its country ministry so poorly, and given it a task so unnecessarily hard, that the appeal of that ministry to the young American of to-day is not strong. The young American desires to be something more than an absentee preacher of sermons. As for foreign missions, the chances are that no likely candidate has heard of such a thing in the twelve or twenty-four times his church has been open during the year. Another explanation may lie in the fact that so many of the country ministers are themselves untrained men. They have experienced religion emotionally and in no other way; and their message is too often a repetition of their personal emotional experience and little else. The more universal message of Christianity based upon the work and the experience of the Church in the Home and the Foreign fields, with its accumulated wealth of social and religious data, its

AN ANCIENT AND PICTURESQUE HOME

service to all sorts and conditions of men, is what the Church and its members find inspiring to-day.

Although the testimony of these untrained leaders, recruited from the ranks of the laity, furnishes inspiration, yet they fail to see the necessity of recruiting others to become professionally trained for tasks which they themselves perform without such training. The South must solve this problem, because an absence of adequate leadership has caused the paralysis of the southern rural church. Moreover, in order to survive, the rural church must be self-sustaining, not only financially, but in developing its own leaders who can best interpret its continuing program. That the pinch of too few ministers is beginning to be felt is shown in the fact that, of the 280 churches, one out of every ten was pastorless at the time of the Survey.

# CHURCH PROGRAM

## The Young People

In the basic counties studied there are only fifty-eight young people's organizations other than Sunday schools. In other words, less than one church out of four has such an organization. In addition to this, three churches have three organizations for boys and six for girls. With great uniformity, ministers and church leaders confessed that their greatest problem was to hold the young people. But the causes of failure are not far to seek. In one of these counties, 55 per cent. of the churches have no Sunday schools; yet some of them have more than 150 active members. This means that in each of these churches with a large membership of adults no provision is made for the religious education of the children who are to be the members and the leaders of the southern church to-morrow.

Many investigators have recorded their impressions of this important problem of the relation of the young folk to the Church. Professor John F. Smith, of Berea College, has presented reliable data bearing on the situation, especially as regards the mountaineers. The young men are simply not reached by the country church and are hostile to it; and responsibility for their attitude rests largely upon the inexperienced, untrained minister. He may reprimand the young folk for their way of amusing themselves; but he offers no constructive program of activities to take the places of those he condemns.

Labored and tedious doctrinal sermons mean nothing to those in the first flush of young manhood and womanhood who naturally desire to live in the throbbing present. They are as frequently alienated by the highly emotional and destructive program of some preachers as they are by the indefinite, austere and unsympathetic attitude of others. The young people whom Professor Smith interviewed frankly expressed the need of a trained ministry. They insisted that the untrained minister is ordained for failure. They look for fewer churches and better programs.

The modern church is vitally concerned with the health and welfare of its young people. This aroused social sense concerns itself with their play as well as with their work. But the recreational contribution of the Southern churches is likewise meager. Scarcely one in five has even an annual Sunday school picnic, which is a time-honored event in the Protestant Church. Only one-tenth of the churches have socials, and less than one-tenth have any other recreational activities. Four churches are interested in co-operating with agricultural and community enterprises, and not quite one in ten has some cultural and educational features in its program. It is natural to find in the South, with its great historic traditions, that national holidays make the chief appeal in varying the normal program. These are observed in sixty-seven, or almost one-fourth, of the churches.

An equal number take part in local charity when the occasion arises; but there is no sociological attitude towards the problem of charity calling for a study, and for sympathetic understanding, of the causes and results. It is merely a kindly, neighborly interest. Only a score of churches undertake any form of missionary service beyond the taking of offerings. Here and there a church supports a native evangelist, and a few others provide for the support of an orphan child each in a church school. One-ninth of the churches engage in union services at irregular intervals.

## The Church Sets Its Par Standard

Throughout this book tentative suggestions are made for the sort of rewarding mission work that should engage the attention of a successful church. Of recent years country church leaders have made various efforts to summarize their ideas as to the reasonable standard for church work. From this effort there finally evolved a so-called "par standard" for country churches. This standard, proposed by the Home Missions Council in collaboration with the rural executives of all denominational Home Mission Boards, was submitted to the Town and Country state supervisors of the Interchurch World Movement.

Virtually all of these men, besides having had executive and survey experience, had been country pastors. Every state in the Union was represented. The par standard was unanimously accepted as a reasonable objective for any country church seeking to fulfill all its obligations. Since that time a number of denominations or synods, districts or associations of denominations, have adopted this standard, with slight modifications, as their own. Among these far-sighted denominations is the Methodist Episcopal Church, South.

To present a summary of the suggestions made in this book, and in order that the people of the region may see how their churches stand in relation to this achievable ideal, the churches of the six basic counties have been graded according to the par standard. The points covered in this standard are listed below.

# CHURCH PROGRAM

The figure in parenthesis after each item indicates the number of churches having this feature, out of the total of 280 churches graded. The items after which no figure appears are those not covered in the schedules used.

## Table

## A Church Measuring Rod

*Adequate Physical Equipment*
Up-to-date parsonage (57)
Adequate church auditorium space (265)
Social and recreational equipment (5)
Well-equipped kitchen
Organ or piano
Separate rooms for Sunday school classes or departments (40)
Stereopticon or motion-picture machine (1)
Sanitary toilets (19)
Horse-sheds or parking space (6)
Property in good repair and condition (225)

*Pastor*
Pastor resident in this parish (49)
Pastor giving full time to this community (14)
Service in this church every Sunday (32)
Minimum salary of $1,200 (95)

*Finance*
Church budget adopted annually (141)
Every member canvass conducted annually (108)
Benevolences equal to 25 per cent. of current expenses (174)

*Meetings*
Coöperation with other churches in same community (34)
Systematic Evangelism (93)

*Parish*
Church serves all Racial and Occupational groups

*Religious Education*
Sunday school held entire year (189)
Sunday school enrollment equal to church membership (82)
Attempt to bring pupils into church membership (97)
Special instruction for church membership (5)
Teacher training or normal class (9)
Provision for leadership training (11)

*Service and Coöperation*
Organized activities for all age and sex groups (27)
Coöperation with boards and denominational agencies (49)
Program adopted annually, 25 per cent. of membership participating
Church reaching entire community

## A Good Southern Example

Centerton, a little open country community of northwest Arkansas, has a Southern Methodist Church whose records prove what can be done when community leadership really awakens to its responsibilities. Farming is the only industry here. The people are all Americans and of fine southern stock. Only two years ago the church was weak, without adequate program or systematic finance, was poorly attended and indifferently sustained. To-day this church is the base of operations in a progressive circuit, with community programs for its combined membership of over 500. When a hurricane blew the Centerton church away last April, plans were immediately laid for a new departmental community building.

Every age and sex group in Centerton village is organized for service. Seventy-five men and boys are enrolled in a large, well-attended athletic club; the girls in the Pollyanna Club have for their interests civic and social improvements; the Boy Scouts are active under the leadership of a live-wire pastor; and the Ladies' Aid Society, with its forty-two members, is a vital force in the community as a women's community club as well as an effective collector of funds for the church. The Centerton church has adopted a systematic method of handling funds; all money is now raised by budget. A Gospel of Neighborliness has brought the people closer together and broken down town and country barriers.

The Sunday school has a seventeen-piece orchestra which is in constant demand for miles around. Study groups and teacher-training classes are held regularly. Every one has his church job; and though many are not members of this community church yet they are ready and willing to line up with the organization and support its program whole-heartedly. Their spirit of coöperation is making the church a strong central influence throughout northwest Arkansas.

This Arkansas story shows in an inspiring way what a country church in the South can do. It shows the progressive tendency among the church leaders of the South. The rapid expansion of summer schools among the Southern Methodists, where men are trained in modern church administration while they derive inspiration for evangelistic and devotional service, must inevitably have a tremendous effect upon the entire South. The Department of Home Missions of the Methodist Episcopal Church, South, is standing for a four-year pastorate, a community-wide survey on which is to be based an extensive evangelistic campaign, at least one service each Sunday for every church, effective pastoral visitation, and a program that shall include every social as well as religious interest in the homes of the community.

# CHURCH PROGRAM

## What a Southern Denomination Plans

Among the other reforms advocated by the Methodist Church, South, are reorganized Sunday schools, missionary and religious societies, adequate provision for recreational and social life, especially through Sunday schools, young people's organizations, and Boy and Girl Scouts. A budget system is outlined for every church with a broad-gauge program of community service. The Board also advocates coöperation with other agencies, secular as well as religious, and for better relations between the races. A program of this kind should receive the support of the denomination, serving as it does almost one-half of the great South, for it is a marked advance in the ways and means of bringing the services of the Church to the rural people of the South.

The same department, under its rural division, is supervising an entire district which is becoming a demonstration point. A score for each church has been worked out and monthly reports are made which are circulated among all the churches. Each church aims to record monthly some definite progress. The score card suggests such matters as a household survey; an evangelistic meeting annually; every-member canvass; use of lay workers; the holding of a rural life institute; attendance by the minister at some rural summer school; and a broad, constructive program for the Sunday school, and for other organizations, which will attract and hold the young people of the South.

# CHAPTER IX

## The Negro Rural Church

S O far we have considered only the white rural church. There are, however, nine million Negroes in the South, three-fourths of whom live in small towns or in the open country. It is estimated that of the Negroes in the open country there are about three million church members. There are no exact data as to the number of Negro churches in the rural South; but the most reliable estimates available place their number at about thirty thousand, and the number of preachers serving these at twenty-five thousand.* It is obvious, therefore, that the Negro rural church cannot be overlooked in this survey.

It should be remembered at the outset that the Negro in America is here through no choice of his own, but as a result of force exercised by the white man for the white man's economic advantage. Nor can one section of the country accuse any other section of sole responsibility for the Negro's presence here. The Negro, therefore, has a peculiar claim upon the white man's interest and sense of obligation.

Moreover, the interests of the two races are essentially at one. Economic welfare, health, sanitation, education, moral character are all essential to safe citizenship for the Negro, just as for any other people. Lacking these essentials, he becomes a handicap, if not a positive peril, to the community in which he lives.

There are the best of reasons, then, why the white man should study the Negro church—the chief source of the Negro's aspiration and the molder of his ideals—in the hope of finding some means of adding to its effectiveness.

On the economic side the Negro has been and is a great asset to the South, furnishing a large part of its labor supply. In particular, he has been invaluable in the cotton field. Recent migrations to the North have been seriously felt in certain parts of the South, from which in some instances whole Negro communities have moved. These migrations have necessarily affected the Negro

* Rev. G. Lake Imes, Dean, Tuskegee Bible Training School.

churches in the South, some of which have lost from one-third to one-half their membership. It is estimated that a half million colored people have taken part in this exodus extending over a period of three or four years.

In the light of the heavy handicap of his background of slavery, the Negro's progress during his sixty years of freedom has been astounding. The figures below, quoted from "The American Survey of the Interchurch World Movement," show the striking contrast between his status in 1860 and his status to-day.

|  | *1860* | *1920* |
|---|---|---|
| Homes owned | 12,000 | 650,000 |
| Farms owned |  | 218,612 |
| Farms owned, acres |  | 13,942,512 |
| Farms owned, value |  | $554,158,000 |
| Farms operated | 20,000 | 926,257 |
| Business enterprises | 2,100 | 60,000 |
| Colleges and normal schools | 15 | 500 |
| College graduates (aggregate) |  | 7,000 |
| Public school teachers | 600 | 30,000 |
| Public school pupils | 100,000 | 2,000,000 |
| Illiteracy | 90 per cent. | 23 per cent. |

Where no migration has taken place there has been a tendency toward a stabilized community life. And where conditions have been favorable, farm and home ownership among the Negroes has greatly increased, in some counties three- or four-fold. This is true in village and town as well as in the country.* Progress is also shown by the small total of petty offenses in those communities in which ownership is increasing and in which, therefore, a pride of home is developing.

The Negro survey was not made in all of the six counties used as the basis for the study of the white churches. The results given here are for three counties only: Harford County, Maryland, representing the Negro under conditions approaching those of the North; Orange County, North Carolina, showing him in a rather isolated development on soil not adapted to cotton raising; and Colbert County, Alabama, most of which lies within the heart of the black belt of the South.. To the results of this survey have been added some data derived from the Census reports, the Bible Training School and Research Department of Tuskegee Institute, and from the Federal Council Commission on the Church and Race Relations. The total Negro population of the three counties for which results are given is 14,157. Of the thirty communities, five-

* Prof. Eugene C. Branson's "Study of the Negro in Orange County, North Carolina."

eighths are growing and a fourth are decreasing in population. The decrease is caused by young people moving North, and those of middle age moving to the towns.

Certain communities have grown because the Negroes have begun to own their own farms, or because higher wages have been paid and Negroes have come in from elsewhere. In both instances, better schools have been established, and have helped to attract Negro settlers. The population has thus become more self-reliant, more independent and better educated in the growing communities than in those in which tenancy prevails or in which the population is decreasing.

A NEGRO SUNDAY SCHOOL

Next to the Church, the school is the most important social institution, and much social life centers in it. Especially in Colbert County, Alabama, and to some extent in the other counties studied, the Negro school situation has improved during the last few years. It is most encouraging to find a broad-minded and ambitious colored woman working as Colored School Supervisor in Colbert County, under the County Superintendent of Schools. Her efforts for the betterment of her race are unfailing.

In this connection it is interesting to note that in the whole South there are 275 of these supervising teachers, visiting regularly 7,850 colored rural schools. These teachers are paid in part by the counties and in part by the Jeanes Fund. The beneficent results of the Rosenwald Fund for the building of model Negro schools and of the John F. Slater Fund for the aid of Negro county training schools are also notable and worthy of study. It should also be borne in mind that the Southern States are constantly raising the level of Negro education by the more generous provision of public funds. This broad policy is reflected in the fact that for the decade between 1910 and 1920 Negro illiteracy in the South decreased from 33.3 per cent. to 26 per cent.

There is a considerable number of religious leaders among these Negroes. Two-thirds of the leaders are farmers, and almost all the rest are ministers or church workers. In eighteen of the thirty communities there is a well-developed community spirit, and in

A CHECKER TOURNAMENT OUTSIDE THE STORE

almost all of the eighteen the schools are good and the proportion of leadership is high. The community spirit manifests itself in the desire for better schools, new school buildings and better pay for teachers, in well-kept homes and in increased efforts to acquire homes.

The Church is not only the most important agency for the moral and religious guidance of the Negroes, but it also contributes largely to their social life. This is especially true in Orange County. Evidence is found in the comparatively small number of fraternal orders among the Negroes, the average being only one and one-half to a community. The total membership of the lodges is only a little more than half as much as the male membership of the Church.

The average attendance, however, is nearly two-thirds of the membership, which is a much larger proportion than is recorded by the white lodges. These counties have fifteen Negro organizations not under church auspices; and it is significant that five of these fifteen concern themselves with school betterment. There are several community clubs and one Mothers' Club.

## The Negro Church of the South

Negro church membership, the number of Negro church organizations, and the value of Negro church property all have shown an amazing increase throughout the South in the last generation. Except in the case of church membership, this increase has been more than 100 per cent. The exclusively Negro denominations, such as the African M. E. Zion and the National Baptist Convention, appear to be growing more rapidly than is the Negro membership of denominations predominantly white.

In the three counties under study, there are seventy-eight Negro churches, eight of them in towns, seventeen in villages and fifty-four in the open country. The Baptists control thirty-eight of these, while five Methodist groups have thirty-four. The other six represent almost as many denominations.

All but five of the churches have buildings. Seventy-two of them are of wooden construction. Two-thirds are in good and five in excellent condition; but the remainder are hardly to be classed as better than poor, or possibly fair. These poorer churches are without paint, or doors, or windows, or general repairs; quite likely the building has not been quite completed. The grounds, too, are sometimes not improved. The seating capacity of these churches averages a little over 300, so that they can seat the church membership three times over, or the population with room to spare. Nine of these buildings are lighted by electricity; the rest use oil lamps. It is most interesting to learn that nine of them have stereopticons and three have moving-picture machines, which is a record twelve times better than that made by the white churches in the six counties studied. Sixty-four of the buildings have only one room each, five have two, and five others have three rooms each. There are twenty-three cemeteries.

The average value of the church buildings is $2,437. Buildings have nearly doubled in value since the Negro churches in Orange County were studied five years ago. The town, village and country churches show nearly the same differences in value as do the city churches. The average Negro town church is worth $4,600, the village church $2,550, the country church $1,530.

## Negro Church Finance

A surprising number of the Negro churches have begun to use the more modern methods of church finance. Twenty of them prepare budgets for all monies, and eleven more for local expense. Only eleven, however, use weekly envelopes and only six conduct an annual every-member canvass. For the most part, these churches are in good financial condition. The total debt is slightly less than

AN AFTERNOON LECTURE AT A NEGRO CHURCH

$2,400, on which from 6 to 8 per cent. interest is paid. The total receipts from the seventy-nine churches amounted in the fiscal year preceding the survey to within a few cents of $42,000. The average town church raised $1,455, the village church $851.76, and the country church $363.66. The average sum per church for the three counties was $644.37. Half the money was raised by subscription, 28 per cent. of it by collection and the rest by miscellaneous methods. Fifty-three per cent. of the money was spent for salaries, 20 per cent. for new buildings and repairs, 12 per cent. for benevolences and 15 per cent. for sundry running expenses.

These contributions represent an average per capita contribution of $9.00 per member. Five years ago the per capita contribution for the Negroes in Orange County was $3.07, and for whites $4. These figures, therefore, show a tremendous increase in the Negro contributions, which have kept pace with the purchasing power of the dollar and established an average within 10 per cent. of the average contribution of the white church members in the six counties.

## Negro Membership

Seven thousand two hundred and seventy-two Negroes belong to the town and country churches in these three counties. Fifteen per cent. of these, or 1,125, are non-resident, so that the churches enroll 43.6 per cent. of the total colored population. Nearly one-third of the resident members are classed as inactive. In this respect the Negro churches show the same tendency that was noted in connection with those of the whites. There are, therefore, 3,636 active members of Negro churches, or 50 per cent. of the total enrollment. Of these active members 1,600 are employed in some gainful occupation. Of the total number of Negro operating farmers, 42 per cent. are church members. Of the total number of Negro tenant farmers, 57 per cent. belong to the churches. It will therefore be seen that the Negro tenant farmers are proportionately far more loyal to their church, or at least far more generally reached by the church, than are the white tenants.

In addition to the active church membership, 538 persons are reported as non-members but nevertheless contributing; and 143 more are in probationary classes looking forward to full church membership. The resident church membership is strongly feminine in its composition, 61 per cent. of it being in this classification. Slightly less than one-third of the females are under twenty-one years of age. Males over twenty-one comprise little more than one-fourth, and those under twenty-one a little more than one-tenth of the total membership. These seventy-eight Negro churches added a total of 645 new members during the last year; but the net gain was only 419, or about 11.2 per cent. of the former net active membership and 6.1 per cent. of the former total membership.

The Negro churches depend almost exclusively upon the evangelistic meeting for the recruiting of church membership. Sixty-four of the churches, including all the stronger ones, hold such meetings for periods of from ten days to two weeks. Four hundred and seventy-two converts were reported, of whom 418 joined the Church. Of other accessions reported, eighty were by confession of faith, and only thirty-seven by letter from other denominations, making a total of 538. Of those who joined the Church on confession, 308 came from the Sunday school.

Approximately one-third of the Negro churches enjoy preaching at least once on Sunday and one-eighth of them have two services on Sunday. Eighteen are on the once-a-month basis. Thirty-three have either two or three services each month.

## Negro Sunday Schools

The Sunday school functions largely in the religious life of the Negroes. Whereas throughout the South one-quarter of the white churches (and throughout the country one-fifth of all the churches) have no Sunday schools, 90 per cent. of the entire number of Negro

NEGRO MEMBERS FIX UP THEIR CHURCH

churches report such schools. All but six of the Negro churches in these counties have Sunday schools, with a total enrollment of 3,746, or an average of fifty-one. The average attendance is thirty-three, or 64 per cent. of the total enrollment. The town schools decidedly lead the others, their average enrollment being seventy, with an average attendance of 74 per cent. The village schools average sixty-two enrolled and thirty-seven attending, or 59 per cent., while those in the country have forty-three on the roll and an attendance of twenty-four, or 56 per cent.

Fifty-two schools, more than two-fifths of the total number, have 165 organized classes. Five use graded lessons, twelve have Cradle Rolls and eight Home Departments. Twenty have more or less regular missionary study and four more than this number give regular missionary offerings. There are nineteen Sunday school libraries. Four schools have social organizations of special or recreational character, and fourteen have regular entertainments for the schools as a whole. Seven of the organized classes hold regular class socials and forty-five schools have the annual picnic. Fifty-six are open during the whole year. Fifteen persons have entered professional Christian service from these Sunday schools in the last decade, and all but one of these within the last five years.

## Church Organizations

Church organizations among the Negroes enroll more than one-half of the net active membership. Women's societies lead with 1,600 members in forty-eight organizations; next in order are the young people's societies, twenty-one in number, with 700 members; and then the girls' societies. The men and boys have nearly half a dozen each. Community life centers in the Negro church to a greater extent than in the white church.

## Church Program

Perhaps the best evidence of life and vision in the Negro church of these southern counties is found in the great interest shown in recent years in church extension in this country as well as in the foreign field, specifically that of Africa. Negro churches give annually hundreds of thousands of dollars for missionary enterprises; and while this Negro contribution does not constitute a very large proportion of American missionary benevolence, yet it indicates an awakening missionary conscience among the members of Negro churches. Thus it is not surprising that five of these churches are supporting native workers in the foreign field. Almost all of the churches celebrate national holidays, anniversaries and festivals. The interest of the Negro in self-improvement is evidenced by the fact that forty-five churches engage in some form of educational or cultural work. This is a higher proportion than has been found among the white churches in any region in America; and it shows the dependence of the Negro upon his church, as well as the way in which he turns to it for self-improvement. Social and recreational features enter into the program of fifteen churches, while ten are taking some interest in civic affairs. Three-fourths are to be depended upon to extend charity within their local communities where it may be needed.

# THE NEGRO RURAL CHURCH

## The Negro Minister

Some observers point out that the Negro preacher is a leader not only in things religious but in the whole round of Negro activities and interests. It is this factor that makes the Negro church so much more of a social center than one would otherwise expect it to be. In a number of welfare campaigns, not only those in connection with the Great War but in those for better sanitation and other community improvements, meetings were held in Negro churches. The Negro preacher's influence extends to economics and his advice is sought even in the details of property transfers and school affairs. He is, not infrequently, the custodian of the association and lodge finances as well as of those of the church. One reason for this is that most of the Negro preachers live with their people.

Fifty-six ordained ministers and one supply serve the seventy-eight colored churches in these three counties. This is a much higher proportion of ordained ministers than is found among the whites. It is true, however, that twenty-six in all, or nearly half these pastors, have other occupations. For the most part, the toiler preacher is a farmer: but two are students, four are teachers, one is a lecturer among his people, and the rest work at odd jobs. Circuits are small and distances traveled are not great. Twenty-seven ministers have but one church each, eighteen have two each, five have three and seven have four each to serve. No minister has more than four churches. The average salary of these ministers amounts to $574.52 a year, which includes the estimated rental value of the parsonages which are furnished for fifteen of these men. The average parsonage value varies greatly in different counties. It is highest in Harford, Maryland, with $646.39; and lowest, $24.17, in Orange, North Carolina, where there is also the highest proportion of ministers having other occupations.

In the matter of salaries, the Federal census reports that in four of the leading Negro denominations the average varies from $247 in those paying the least, to $350 in the best paying denomination. Figures furnished by the Federal Council Commission, derived from a study of five counties in Arkansas and Georgia, show a salary average of about $600 for the preachers reported on; and it may safely be assumed that these were the better paid men.

No study of the training of Negro preachers was made in the districts under survey; but some interesting and valuable data on this point have been furnished by the Federal Council Commission and by the Biblical and Research Departments of Tuskegee. In two Arkansas counties, where inquiries were conducted by the Federal Council Commission, ten out of sixty-three colored preachers reported graduation from high school or college. In one Georgia county, admittedly above the average in this respect, twelve out of thirty-one reported high school or more advanced preparation; but in another county of the same state only one out of sixteen was so reported, while eleven were reported as without training in any school.

The estimates furnished by Tuskegee for the entire South place the average lower, rating probably not more than 1 per cent. of Negro preachers as college graduates and 3 per cent. as high school graduates. Regarding the apparent discrepancy between this estimate and the other figures, it may be explained that different classifications of schools probably were used, and that while the Tuskegee estimate refers to graduation, the other figures may have been based on partial completion of high school and college courses.

In the matter of special ministerial training five Arkansas and Georgia counties, having a total of 145 colored preachers, reported eleven of them, or about 7.5 per cent., as having had some measure of theological training. This figure corresponds closely with the Tuskegee estimate that only 5 per cent. have had any systematic professional training.

Commenting on this whole educational situation, Dr. George E. Haynes, of the Federal Council Commission, points out "the encouraging fact that ministers and people are beginning to realize to a considerable degree that there must be at least a showing of preparation on the part of the minister," and that in a number of the cases studied the ministers were intellectually qualified for their work.

Regarding absentee pastors the Federal Council office affords the information that in the five Arkansas and Georgia counties just referred to, only about one-fourth of the rural Negro pastors lived within their respective parishes. "The rule to which there are but few exceptions in the case of the absentee minister," we are told, "is that the minister lives in a large town or city, comes out to the once-a-month church on Saturday evening or Sunday morning, holds a class meeting or testimony meeting Saturday night, follows this with a service lasting nearly all day on Sunday, and leaves Monday morning for home, to be seen no more until the next 'meetin' day.'"

The facts brought out in this study reveal clearly certain outstanding needs of the Negro rural church; and the chapter would not be complete without some constructive suggestions as to how these needs may be met, and particularly as to what white churches and religious leaders may do to help.

What is most needed is a better-trained ministry. This may be provided by the strengthening of Negro schools in general, and especially by more generous support of colleges and theological seminaries by the educational and mission boards of the white denominations. Most of the latter are already doing something along this line, but the aggregate is far short of the need. They might well consider, also, the desirability of a concerted program and coordinated effort in this field. The churches might interest themselves as well in the general question of popular Negro education, first finding out the facts and then bringing influence to bear in the interest of whatever improvement appears to be needed and practicable.

Another practical plan, which has already been adopted by some of the southern white denominations, is that of providing summer schools or conferences for Negro preachers, and making attendance possible by the furnishing of financial aid. One denomination in the South holds two such schools annually, reaching several hundred colored preachers with a stiff ten-days' program.

In a number of communities, notably in Chattanooga, Tennessee, the colored preachers have been invited to membership in the local ministerial associations. The results have been excellent, not only as affording encouragement and help to the colored preachers, but also by way of unifying the Christian forces of the community. There would seem to be no reason why this plan might not be generally adopted with mutual profit.

In antebellum days it was a common thing for white preachers to occupy Negro pulpits. The practice might well be revived as opportunity offers, not in order, as one southern writer puts it, "to give the Negro patronizing advice," but to give him the benefit of the white man's highest religious ideals, and to enlist his sympathetic coöperation toward their realization. The interchange of pulpits may not often be practicable in the South; but it might sometimes be effected with profit in the way of fuller understanding and sympathy.

Negro choirs, quartettes and soloists may be asked occasionally to sing in white churches. This has been done in some of the largest and most conservative churches in the South and has proved quite popular, especially when the Negro "spirituels" are sung with their characteristic beauty and pathos. In many neglected districts, Negro Sunday schools might be organized in which consecrated white men and women would find opportunity for a much needed and most Christlike ministry, to the mutual benefit of both teachers and pupils.*

* The above suggestions are not offered as from the outside, but summarize the considered opinions of a number of southern leaders before whom the results of the Survey were laid.

# CHAPTER X

## Conclusions

THIS study of the Church and of church life in the South ought not to be left without some statement of conclusions and recommendations. The facts assembled in this volume were reported by the churches themselves. The conclusions and recommendations that follow are presented, by those responsible for the investigation, for what they are worth and as expressing the views of outsiders. They have, however, been approved in the main by a number of southern leaders to whom they have been submitted. Many of the suggestions that follow have also been made in another form by the Rural Department of the Board of Missions of the Methodist Episcopal Church, South.

### Intangible Possessions

An evaluation of the country church in the South must take into account certain of the Church's intangible possessions. The overwhelming majority of the population in the South is Protestant. The Church does not face a constituency whose traditions and feelings are either hostile or indifferent to its appeal. The loyalty to the Church of those making up its membership is based on a whole-hearted emotional commitment of individuals to the religion for which the Church stands. It lies, therefore, within the power of the Church to lead the people. This was shown during the war when the draft law could be explained to communities in certain sections only through the Church. Nowhere else did this situation arise. Here are intangible possessions of great value to organized religion.

Further, it should be noted that the South is, more markedly perhaps than any other part of America, a region of contrasts. The southern fringe of the mountain counties lie but little more than an overnight journey from the sophisticated prosperity of the orange growers of Florida. In some cases there are within the same county communities as alert and progressive as any in America, with all the machinery of twentieth century community life and organization, and other communities where conditions are almost as they were in the reconstruction days that followed the Civil War.

A contrast just as striking is presented in southern educational affairs. Per capita expenditures per pupil in different states and even in different counties within the same state vary by hundreds of per cent. The progressive communities are assets and show what can be done. In the selection of the six basic counties of this study the effort was made to choose those which would show the

UNCLE SAM SPREADS THE NEWS TO THE MOUNTAINS

direction in which the South was tending. Similarly, in these recommendations, nothing has been suggested which more progressive churches in the rural South are not either doing or attempting.

## Evangelism

Evangelism is the greatest function of the Church. It is the keynote of the southern religious program. It has yielded, however, uneven results. In the first place the Church record shows a very high proportion of inactive members. When virtually one-fourth of the members no longer attend or contribute, it is fair to conclude that evangelism has before it an unfinished task. How uneven the results of evangelism have been is shown by the fact

# CONCLUSIONS

that church membership in different counties within the region and even of communities within adjoining counties varies from 5 per cent. to over 50 per cent. of the population. Obviously the evangelistic effort of the churches has been either unequally distributed or unequally effectual. Either the effort must be exerted effectually in more communities or other methods must be found for unresponsive localities. The outstanding suggestion of the Survey is that there be a greater and a better evangelism, one which shall leave no age- or sex-group untouched, which shall overlook no social or economic class; an evangelism that will add to the triumph of conversion the sustained program that will bring new converts to the church both to have and to hold.

## Household Survey

Apart from the spiritual groundwork, the best way to prepare for successful evangelism is by conducting a household survey of the community, or, in other words, by taking a religious census. Such a survey is often successfully made for the pastor, under his direction, by the organizations in his church. It may be made by the men's clubs or women's clubs or by the young people's organizations, or by apportioning the canvass among all the units. Often, however, the pastor of a small group of churches will have to do the work himself. It will be worth while. Blanks for the purpose may be obtained from various sources; but it is best for the minister to get his from denominational headquarters, which can furnish both blanks and advice. Where possible, such a survey should be by all the churches in a given community; but if that is not possible and one church takes the initiative, denominational courtesies ought to be exchanged. For instance, surveyors who find any non-church-going members of a sister denomination ought to send the names of these to the pastor of their denomination or to the pastor of the denomination for which preference may be expressed. Moreover, the household survey, judiciously managed, has several important by-products. It enables the preacher to discover what the people are thinking about the church, its functions and opportunities. It makes possible agreement on a program of church work in which members old and new may be enlisted. This is especially valuable, because that program is best for a church which the church builds for itself out of a knowledge of its own situation. Such a practice does more to conserve evangelistic results than anything else; it furnishes a proper outlet for roused emotion;

95

and furnishes the contacts and the information by which the church can be linked more closely to the community it is serving.

## The Minister and His Pastorate

Splendid as has been the lay leadership in many local churches in the South, the real key to the situation is the minister. The Survey shows that the average minister has from two to six churches, necessitating much travel, and that he stays but two years with his charge. The chief function of the minister is preaching. The salary is often meager. Dr. Masters in his book, "The Country Church in the South," quotes two successful pastors of the Baptist denomination as rejoicing that their sons were not entering the ministry. The southern denominations are awake to the situation. The suggestions here made are in harmony with the policy advocated by many of their leaders.

The denominations should take advantage of better roads and transportation, wherever possible, to reduce the number of churches on circuits by consolidating congregations. There is no excuse for the large number of overlapping parishes of churches of the same denomination. Fewer churches would mean less travel, more intensive and more satisfactory service and better results. The whole problem of the circuit arrangement of churches should be scientifically studied from the point of view of ministerial service. Some arresting instances of unnecessary travel have been discovered. Three ministers of the same denomination living within a seven-mile radius traveled 534 miles, going and coming, to preach to three churches all within a five-mile radius and connected by good roads. Several instances of a minister traveling over 400 miles, round trip, for a single service were discovered. Extreme cases these; but they call attention impressively to something it should not be difficult to correct. Nor can this circuit problem be studied without regard to the growing tendency of the village churches to avail themselves of the full time of a resident pastor, thereby throwing the weaker, outlying country points on their own resources. Since an additional pastor is needed, in such instances, it would be well to experiment, to try holding the old circuit together and employing an additional worker or assistant pastor.

The rearrangement of circuits will help toward another desideratum, the longer pastorate. Many are coming to see the need of this. If it is true that in many communities the tenant farmer is one of the chief causes of disturbing social conditions, what shall be said of the ministerial sojourner?

# CONCLUSIONS

The southern rural pastor is as impermanent as his tenant parishioner. Careful study of the Methodist Church, South, showed that its pastors stayed, on the average, only two years in each parish. In 1920, according to data derived from the Federal Census, 20.1 per cent., or one in every five persons operating farms in the South, whether as owners or as tenants, had been on the same farm less than one year.

The church ought to take a stand for longer pastorates. Two to three years do not give time for a pastor, however gifted and inspired, to become acquainted with the problems of his church and his parishioners. With the comings and goings of pastors as well as of members of the flock and with the vacant intervals between pastorates, the rural church in the South does not justify its service. Elsewhere in America, where a pastorate lasts longer than four years, the results in every department justify the longer investment of time by one man in one church.

Perhaps the ideal plan in the South as well as elsewhere is to have a full-time resident minister for every congregation of one hundred or more active members. This will be impossible, however, for many years to come. The people cannot support such a program, and there are not enough ministers. Hence the importance of the considerations urged; for in ways indicated, existing man power can be utilized for greater production and the job itself be made more attractive to the man.

The question of compensation is still to be considered; and here there is a vicious circle. Where a church receives meager service it pays a meager salary. Where a pastor is handicapped by a meager salary, he either moves to a more remunerative parish or he abandons the Church and takes up a secular occupation. Yet no country churches are more generous than those of the South when they do receive full-time service. A dozen of the 181 ministers in the six basic counties are receiving salaries of between $2,000 and $3,000. On the other hand, sixty-three are busy with other occupations in addition to the ministry. Only by an educational campaign reaching both the pastors and the people will the progressive denominational leaders show the evils attendant on this division of effort.

## Religious Education

In the sphere of religious life and progress, as well as in the field of social improvement, education is of the greatest importance.

# CHURCH LIFE IN THE RURAL SOUTH

The present may be unable to realize its ideals; but it can teach these ideals and make them the practice of the future. Nowhere would this procedure be of more importance than in the rural church of the South. The practice of some of the denominations of holding conferences, summer assemblies and retreats is to be commended, though these too seldom draw from the rural churches. The sending of deputations to churches in order that by demonstration they may learn better working methods is of greater value. The South must in some way reach all within its local congregations who can lead; the minister must find and use them in a great local effort of religious education, as the Y. M. C. A. county work secretary finds and uses his leaders. The central feature of the religious educational program is the Sunday school; but only three out of every four churches have such an organization. Many existing Sunday schools are open only a part of the year. Many provide activities only of the most elementary sort. They lack graded lessons, organized classes, a social program. Most of them even omit the Sunday school picnic. Church after church in this Survey reported the future bright except for the problem of holding the young people. If the future is bright without the Sunday school, how much brighter that future would be if the Sunday school were included in each church program! The Sunday school is the reservoir of church membership and leadership. A great advance in education has been made in the United States since the World War, with the utilization of modern apparatus. Instruction by the use of the stereopticon, the moving-picture screen, and the blackboard should become a matter of denominational concern; and such apparatus ought to be sent on tour among the churches that cannot own them.

Cradle Rolls, Home Departments, organized classes with graded lessons, are within the reach of all churches. Each should also have a teachers' training class and a Workers' Council or Cabinet of Religious Education coöperating with the pastor and superintendent for Sunday school improvement. There are now many devices, inexpensive and yet artistic, which make it possible to separate and equip classes even in a one-room building.* These could be used to advantage.

* See "The Sunday School at Work in Town and Country," by M. W. Brabham, General Sunday School Board, Methodist Episcopal Church, South. Published by George H. Doran Co., New York.

# CONCLUSIONS

## Equipment

A program such as is here indicated could be helped by a larger equipment than the average church possesses. Even the one-room building will admit of some improvement. The devices for separating classes have already been mentioned. Sand tables and good pictures would help when the leadership can use them. A stereopticon would be a great asset. One could be purchased coöperatively by the churches of a circuit. In all the counties studied there is not a church that has a playground and there are virtually no parish or community houses. As roads are improved and travel is made enough easier to allow the consolidation of two or more churches of the same denomination, such consolidations ought to be made, in many cases, and playgrounds and parish or community houses provided.

In some few centers, perhaps in one in each ecclesiastical unit, one church of outstanding ability or strategic position might provide full equipment and enter into the fullest possible program of activities. Such a church would become not only a demonstration point, but also an experiment station. Its successes and its mistakes alike would be valuable.

## Organizations

In this day of complicated social standards the value to a church of organized age- and sex-groups is incalculable; these organizations for the young and for the adults form the membership into a flexible and cohesive body and help to interpret the church program to the community at large. Through such organizations the church offers its coöperation to agencies like the Red Cross, the Sunday School Association, the Young Men's Christian Association and the Young Women's Christian Association, and to such officials as the County Superintendent of Education, the County Farm Demonstration and Home Economic Agents and to public-spirited organizations that are fighting the battle for health and sanitation.

But in no other part of the United States has the country church so meager a program of church work as in the South. In the southern country church there are very few groups or specialized organizations. The lack of organized groups of young people has already been noted. Among women, who elsewhere in America constitute the steady church workers, the lack of organization is especially felt. Nor is the new interest in church administration that is being generally shown by the men evident in the southern rural church. These will come only when a pastor stays long enough in his parish to organize the church and link it with the life of the community.

## Program

The analysis of the church program in the counties studied throughout the South shows that preaching is regarded as the church's only function. But a larger program does not minimize preaching; it really illustrates the spoken word in avenues that connect the church with the life of the community. The sick body and the sick mind are of importance as well as the sick soul which they effect. Sermons, like crops, should be diversified. And they should contain a larger message fraught with solace for the sick of body, of mind and of soul.

Especially should the effort be made to have every church open every Sunday, whether there is a preaching service or not. The Sunday school, particularly if its program be enlarged and vitalized, can contribute much. The young people's society can also help. But outside its usual work and machinery, the Church has missed a part of its obligation to serve the community in those broad ways that make life more worth living. One of the real dangers of the southern country church is at this point.

It is permitting the various welfare agencies to capitalize the quickened interest of the people, to win their allegiance to eminently worth-while programs—programs which could best be developed by the social institutions already in the community, namely the church and the school. The people themselves are beginning to see this. The field worker who visited five of the six counties and spent nearly four months in the South, attending from two to five services a Sunday, did not hear a single sermon from any pulpit which was not doctrinal in character. During the entire journey within these counties there was no word from any Christian pulpit of any denomination with which the field worker worshiped that stressed the ethics of Jesus as applied to the level of the everyday life which people have to live. This is not to say that the experience of the field worker is of universal application in the South, nor is it to decry doctrine: every church must have a well-thought out philosophy of Christianity; but theology and philosophy are not the whole of life or of the religion of Jesus Christ. That which the Church could have furnished is now coming from other

## CONCLUSIONS

4 5 2 2 6

sources. The failure of the Church to do all that it might is patent in the figures that have been given in this book, figures supplied by the churches themselves. It is to be questioned whether the Church can reach with its theology those who are now beyond its influence, unless it brings a gospel applied in understandable terms to the life which they are living. One of the biggest questions for the southern country church to-day is whether it will oppose the community movement, trail after it, or lead it.

It is suggested, therefore, that in every parish a community program should be outlined to deal with the more important of such questions as these—better roads; better housing; better living conditions; better schools and agriculture; the care of the sick, the indigent and the feeble-minded; elimination of centers of vice and moral infection. At least one rural life institute dealing with such topics might be held each year. On the constructive side, there should be provision for adequate and wholesome amusement for age- and sex-groups. The Church should take an interest in everything that is of interest to the people to which it ministers, for there is nothing which the people do that does not relate itself to their spiritual life. It is often not necessary for the Church to do anything more along this line than to offer its coöperation to such agencies as the Red Cross, the Sunday School Association, the Young Men's Christian Association, the Young Women's Christian Association, and to such officials as the County Superintendent of Education, and County Farm Demonstration and Home Economic Agent. Sometimes, however, it must be an actual leader.

### Finance

The suggestions here made regarding improvement and enlarged program raise the question of finance. It is raised also by the need of denominational boards to secure funds for the maintenance and development of work at home and abroad. Considering the amount of pastoral service which the churches in the South get, the financial response of the membership is quite good; and any considerable increase in finance will probably depend on increased leadership. Still, the records of those churches whose finances have been arranged in accordance with systems that have proved efficient indicate that the churches lacking such systems could materially increase their resources and the treasuries of their missionary organizations if they would resort to the every-member canvass, budget and envelope system.

If the churches without these mere mechanical devices used by a wise minority would adopt them and use them with equal skill, the money to pay for the equipment and activities suggested here would soon be forthcoming.

## Other Considerations

So much for the task of the Church in its usual and accepted field of work. There remain certain other considerations. Some of these must be passed over with a word because they did not lie within the original scope of this study of rural church life in the South.

The South led the country in the advance toward national prohibition and the churches of the South played their good part. Along with every agency of law and order everywhere in America, the church of the South ought to stand for obedience to the law of the land. Since the completion of the field work of this investigation in the spring of 1921, the Ku Klux Klan has been enormously expanded. This organization was not, however, a factor in the life of any of the counties at the time of the investigation. Then there is the Negro problem. The suggestions of southern leaders themselves on this question have already been offered in Chapter IX. The South understands the Negro, his economic importance in the new era that is opening; and southern white leaders are coöperating with southern Negro leaders in an honest policy of good will and understanding. The Commission on Interracial Coöperation is a well-known medium for arriving at this understanding so necessary for the well-being of the two races. But the dominating influence in the situation lies with the Church. The two races, irrespective of color, share in common the privileges of Christian democracy. Southern leaders must not fail to recognize that strong, well-organized, community-serving churches, for the white as well as for the black people, will prove the essential helps along the new industrial road to which the South is setting its feet. A Church with a racial problem in its community should consult the Commission on Interracial Coöperation, Atlanta, Ga.

Beyond these considerations are still others of a large nature on which the Survey did secure data and of which it may speak.

## The Economic Situation

In the South more than in any other section of America agriculture and the type of life it brings have overwhelmingly predominated. That a period of economic transition is now impending, a period of gradual or accelerated transition from the agricultural to industrial, is evident in this survey and from an examination of census figures. Such changes cannot but influence considerably the religious and social institutions which are the very strength and genius of southern life. The leaders of the South can so guide these natural processes of economic development that the more violent social and religious dislocations, familiar in the communities of New England and the Middle West, can be avoided. To this end the Church and the social and educational agencies must be employed to the fullest extent.

A PROSPEROUS FARM IN ORANGE COUNTY, NORTH CAROLINA

These economic and social transitions are inevitably felt by the Church. The time has now come when the leaders of the South will turn to the Church and its many agencies for guidance and coöperation. Economic and social problems, the ravages of nature and disease, the contacts and interactions of country and city life, are vital questions with which the southern Church must concern itself; and nowhere will these questions present themselves more insistently than in the rural communities.

Because of the urgency of its economic situation the southern Church must give this question consideration. In modern life the Church is an economic factor and an integral part of our economy. Times of plenty and times of scarcity are both reflected in the Church and strengthen or hamper it in its work. The rural Church in the South has a real interest in the economic welfare and future of the farmer. When a farmer who is a church member loses $3,000 in a year on his cotton because of the ravages of the boll weevil, or when the savings of a life-time are destroyed by the work of the same insect, or by the fluctuations of the cotton market, the Church shares in these disasters.

It behooves the country Church to identify itself with the economic life of its congregations and to become an educational factor in the various campaigns to improve conditions. The Church should open its pulpit to the preachers of the new agriculture. It may also disseminate knowledge of an economic nature. Should the South, for instance, enter rapidly into such crop diversification as would result in an overproduction of corn in competition with the Middle West, social and religious institutions in both these regions would suffer.

In an economic problem nearer home, like that created by the tenant farmer, the Church can exert a stabilizing influence. Already the tenant farmer has weakened the Church because, a transient, he has displaced an element of the population that was abiding. He shifts from farm to farm, from one community to another. As Professor Branson's study shows, this type of tenancy produces illiteracy, and in its turn illiteracy creates tenancy. As tenancy increases among white farmers the ratios of church membership fall, and the Sunday school, which is the reservoir of membership, loses vitality and recruits. Economically, the church should be more concerned with the problem of reaching the tenant farmer and attaching him to the community by more lasting bonds, than it should be with the problem of reaching the owner operator. In any case, since the Church ministers to both these types in its membership, it should perform the important mission of interpreting the one to the other. Until the Church can make conditions of tenancy more favorable, the transient tenant will hold himself aloof from church life as well as from community life.

A page from the program of the mission church in a great agricultural country like India may furnish suggestions for the southern tenant problem. Here the mission church improves the term of tenancy, or interprets the rural credit system to the tenant so that he can purchase on favorable terms. While this suggestion comes from a distant field, it shows that the Church may serve the farmer tenant and the landlord in its membership in a way to give impetus to associations of tenants and owners, or farmers in general, independent of the Church, but composed of church members.

The Church cannot, however, fill this great rôle until it has become in the community a social and religious power to which men turn with their differences and troubles. It must bind itself to every member of its congregation, whether a struggling tenant or a prosperous land-owner, by intimate ties of loyalty and service. When the tenant farmer feels that he can derive moral and economic support from the Church in improving his working and living conditions; when the landowner feels that a tenant member in his church is the sort of person to whom he can entrust his land, or sell his land upon reasonable terms, then the Church has become a real community factor. Moreover, until such ties are established,

ONCE A CROSSROAD STORE

A church made a club house out of this deserted building

until the tenant feels that his living and working environment is favorable, that his children are receiving the benefits of a full, well-balanced program in the Sunday school, he will remain a disturbing force in southern community life.

Especially must the Church be forearmed because, as the new industrial era of the South develops, the tenants may largely disappear in some communities, may be driven to or become attracted by the growing industrial centers with their better wages and their crowded living conditions. In this event the agricultural South and its institutions may face a serious situation.

# CHURCH LIFE IN THE RURAL SOUTH

## Good Roads

Of the churches covered by this investigation, from two-thirds to three-quarters reported poor roads as one of the chief causes of low attendance and membership. But the Church is a community institution, officially tax-free because any and all may share its religious and social services. If bad roads interfere with the rendering of these services, then the Church may well lead in the movement for road improvement. If the question of a bond issue for highway betterment arises, the influence of a public institution like the Church is incalculable. None is a better judge of the evil results of bad roads than is the pastor: his flock cannot regularly reach the church, and he visits his flock with difficulty. What more inspiring example than that of the Alsatian pastor, John Frederick Oberlin, who with pick and shovel began constructing the road that revolutionized the life of his little community!

Good roads are of still greater importance. They link communities, they enlarge community boundaries, they make consolidation of schools and churches possible. When, for instance, roads enlarge communities, one church can often do the work of two. Larger congregations are formed, with a natural increase of social and religious activities. Then the pastor will receive adequate support, and stay long enough to do constructive parochial work.

## Health

Jesus said: "Heal the sick." While the Church has a definite share in social and religious problems, it cannot directly care for the sick. The pastor will always, however, bring to the bedside of his parishioner the consolations of religion. But the social responsibility of the Church to the community in all that concerns spiritual and moral welfare includes matters like those of health and sanitation. Ignorance leads to suffering, and it is through the publicity of school and church that a campaign for better health is most successful. The ravages of the hookworm disease in the southern mountains and elsewhere are lessening as a result of proper treatment and preventative measures. The need of sanitation and of the reduction of the high typhoid rate in many a southern county presents a task for the Church. The Church cannot enter into a public health campaign: but it can coöperate by giving publicity, approval and the weight of its prestige to all movements that aim to improve the public health and the social well-being. During the

106

War, it successfully coöperated with agencies like the Red Cross; and it should continue to keep in touch with all such agencies.

## Education

From one community interest, the Church goes to another. None is more important than that of good schools. It is impossible to overemphasize the value of these to the South. He who is illiterate is not fulfilling his duty as an American citizen. An illiterate can hardly be urged to search the Scriptures. The schools

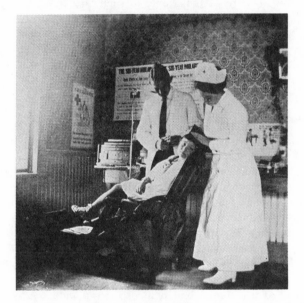

A RURAL CLINIC

not only make for a better democracy but through them is also developed the responsive intelligence to which the Church can appeal, and through which the Church can most effectively interpret its social and religious message. They are indispensable adjuncts to the Sunday school. In many cases good schools for his children solve the tenant farmer's problem. But the schools in the South are too often the victims of board politics. A teacher should be appointed for her ability to teach instead of because of her influence with the school board. Moreover, the teacher should not suffer discrimination because of her denominational belief.

107

Colbert County furnishes an example in point which should be followed throughout the South. Its story should be told wherever possible. In this county the people themselves, under the leadership of the County Superintendent of Schools, have risen to provide better education for their children. They have so greatly improved their schools that one comparing those of to-day with those of five years ago would feel that here a miracle had been wrought. Public opinion is being created which permits country boys and country girls to continue their studies longer than used to be customary. More than this, the school has become a community servant, has entered into the life of the people to such an extent that much of the social activity of the community centers upon this institution which the people themselves finance and therefore own. A notable increase in community spirit has resulted, and the people have developed a far more intelligent interest in the future of the county and the county's most valuable assets, her boys and girls.

## Interchurch Cooperation

No one church can do all the things that have been suggested in these conclusions. In one community one need is outstanding; and in a neighboring community, another. As has been said, that church and that community is most fortunate whose program can be locally developed and executed. But the suggestions made here offer real tasks for the Church, and progress will be most rapid if there can be some Interchurch coöperation.

Religious problems cannot be solved without an exchange of information by the religious bodies concerned, without conferences and coöperation. If loyalty to a denominational organization interferes with loyalty to the Kingdom of God, a kind of rivalry will ensue in which the people will be neglected and forgotten. Interchurch coöperation has lagged in the South for many reasons which need not be discussed here. Individualism, small congregations, itinerant preachers zealous to keep up their own organizations, are a few of the causes. The time of coöperation has now come if the country church of the South is to forge ahead. This coöperation can be both local and on a county basis. Luckily it can create a Christian community program without regard to denominational lines, which so far as worship goes may be kept separate. Beginnings have already been made to work this, but on a county basis. County Sunday school associations are numerous in the South. Colbert County had, until the financial depression, a county council of religious education with a paid secretary which was bringing together most of the church members in a broad-gauge program of leadership, training, religious education and health, as well as of missionary activities, in the less favored sections of the county.

The greatest obstacles to progress along this line, as along the line of elimination of overchurching, are the ministers themselves. They hold the future in their hands. If they rise to the opportunity made theirs by the influence the Church now holds in the South, the country church in the South will have a remarkable future. If they fail to grasp this opportunity the Church may be superseded and the enlarged program for which it might be responsible may pass to the hands of the others.

A keen observer says: "Religion in the South is infinitely puzzling. It is a paradox, dead and yet alive, unprogressive and narrow but a powerful force." The future of the country church in the South depends upon how this force is directed in the years that are just ahead.

APPENDICES

# APPENDIX I

## Methodology and Definitions

THE method used in the Town and Country Surveys of the Interchurch World Movement and of those of the Committee on Social and Religious Surveys differs from the method of earlier surveys in this field chiefly in the following particulars:

1. "Rural" was defined as including all population living outside of incorporated places of over 5,000. Previous surveys usually excluded all places of 2,500 population or over, which follows the United States Census definition of "rural."

2. The local unit for the assembling of material was the community, regarded usually as the trade area of a town or village center. Previous surveys usually took the minor civil division as the local unit. The disadvantage of the community unit is that census and other statistical data are seldom available on that basis, thus increasing both the labor involved and the possibility of error. The great advantage is that it presents its results assembled on the basis of units which have real social significance, which the minor civil division seldom has. This advantage is considered as more than compensating for the disadvantage.

3. The actual service area of each church, as indicated by the residence of its members and adherents, was mapped and studied. This was an entirely new departure in rural surveys.

Four chief processes were involved in the actual field work of these surveys:

1. The determination of the community units and of any subsidiary neighborhood units included within them. The community boundaries were ascertained by noting the location of the last family on each road leading out from a given center who regularly traded at that center. These points, indicated on a map, were connected with each other by straight lines. The area about the given center thus enclosed was regarded as the community.

2. The study of the economic, social and institutional life of each community as thus defined.

113

3. The location of each church in the county, the determination of its parish area and the detailed study of its equipment, finance, membership, organization, program and leadership.

4. The preparation of a map showing, in addition to the usual physical features, the boundaries of each community, the location, parish area and circuit connections of each church and the residence of each minister.

The following are the important definitions used in the making of these surveys and the preparation of the reports:

## Geographical

City—a center of over 5,000 population. Not included within the scope of these surveys except as specifically noted.

Town—a center with a population of from 2,501 to 5,000.

Village—a center with a population of from 251 to 2,500.

Hamlet—any clustered group of people not living on farms, whose numbers do not exceed 250.

Open Country—the farming area, excluding hamlets and other centers.

Country—used in a three-fold division of population included in scope of survey into Town, Village and Country. Includes Hamlets and Open Country.

Town and Country—the whole area covered by these surveys, i.e., all population living outside of cities.

Rural—used interchangeably with Town and Country.

Community—that unit of territory and of population characterized by common social and economic interests and experiences; an "aggregation of people the majority of whose interests have a common center." Usually ascertained by determining the normal trade area of each given center. The primary social grouping of sufficient size and diversity of interests to be practically self-sufficing in ordinary affairs of business, civil and social life.

Neutral Territory—any area not definitely included within the area of one community. Usually an area between two or more centers and somewhat influenced by each, but whose interests are so scattered that it cannot definitely be assigned to the sphere of influence of any one center.

Neighborhood—a recognizable social grouping having certain interests in common but dependent for certain elemental needs upon some adjacent center within the community area of which it is located.

# APPENDIX I

Rural Industrial—pertaining to any industry other than farming within the Town and Country area.

## Population

Foreigner—refers to foreign-born and native-born of foreign parentage.

New Americans—usually includes foreign-born and native-born of foreign or mixed parentage, but sometimes refers only to more recent immigration. In each case the exact meaning is clear from the context.

## The Church

Parish—the area within which the members and regular attendants of a given church live.

Circuit—two or more churches combined under the direction of one minister.

Resident Pastor—a church whose minister lives within its parish area is said to have a resident pastor.

Full-time Resident Pastor—a church with a resident pastor who serves no other church and follows no other occupation than the ministry is said to have a full-time resident pastor.

Part-time Pastor—a church whose minister either serves another church also, or devotes part of his time to some regular occupation other than the ministry, or both, is said to have a part-time minister.

Non-Resident Member—one carried on the rolls of a given church but living too far away to permit regular attendance; generally, any member living outside the community in which the church is located unless he is a regular attendant.

Inactive Member—one who resides within the parish area of the church but who neither attends its services nor contributes to its support.

Net Active Membership—the resultant membership of a given church after the number of non-resident and inactive members is deducted from the total on the church roll.

Per Capita Contributions or Expenditures—the total amount contributed or expended divided by the number of the *net active* membership.

Budget System—A church which at the beginning of the fiscal year makes an itemized forecast of the entire amount of money required for its maintenance during the year as a basis for a canvass of its membership for funds is said to operate on a budget system with respect to its local finances. If amounts to be raised for denominational or other benevolences are included in the forecast and canvass, it is said to operate on a budget system for all moneys raised.

Adequate Financial System—Three chief elements are recognized in an adequate financial system: a budget system, an annual every-member canvass and the use of envelopes for the weekly payment of subscriptions.

Receipts—Receipts have been divided under three heads:

*a.* Subscriptions, that is, money received in payment of annual pledges.

*b.* Collections, that is, money received from free-will offerings at public services.

*c.* All other sources of revenue, chiefly proceeds of entertainments and interest on endowments.

Salary of Minister—Inasmuch as some ministers receive in addition to their cash salary the free use of a house, while others do not, a comparison of the cash salaries paid is misleading. In all salary comparisons, therefore, the cash value of a free parsonage is arbitrarily rated as $250 a year and that amount is added to the cash salary of each white minister with free parsonage privileges. Thus an average salary stated as $1,450 is equivalent to $1,200 cash and the free use of a house.

# APPENDIX II

## Bibliography

THE complete bibliography covering the southern area and particularly the six counties under consideration would consume too much space to be given here. Local newspapers, church diaries, county records and reports and many similar sources of information were consulted. The Federal Census reports from 1890 to date and the reports of the United States Bureau of Education were also used, as were the State Reports on Education on agriculture, health, education, road building, etc. The *Weekly News Letter* of the University of North Carolina proved especially valuable, as did the annual publication of the University Club at that institution. Special mention, however, should be made of the following articles or books of recent origin:

"The South and the New Citizenship."

*The Survey*—entire issue of April 3, 1920.

"The Southern Highlander and His Homeland," John C. Campbell, Russell Sage Foundation, 1921.

"Our Southern Highlanders," Horace Kephart, Macmillan Company, 1921.

Bulletin on the Church and Landless Men, University of North Carolina.

"Rural Child Welfare," Edward Clopper, Macmillan Company, 1922.

Reports of the Social and Political Congress.

Reports of the Southern Sociological Congress.